NAVIGATING TREACHEROUS WATERS

A State Takeover Handbook

Liam J. Garland

A SCARECROWEDUCATION BOOK

The Scarecrow Press, Inc.
Lanham, Maryland, and Oxford
2003

A SCARECROWEDUCATION BOOK

Published in the United States of America
by Scarecrow Press, Inc.
A Member of the Rowman & Littlefield Publishing Group
4720 Boston Way, Lanham, Maryland 20706
www.scarecroweducation.com

PO Box 317
Oxford
OX2 9RU, UK

British Library Cataloguing in Publication Information Available

Library of Congress Cataloging-in-Publication Data
Garland, Liam J. (Liam James), 1973–
  Navigating treacherous waters : a state takeover handbook / Liam J. Garland.
     p. cm.
"A ScarecrowEducation book."
Includes bibliographical references and index.
  ISBN 0-8108-4611-X (pbk. : alk. paper)
  1. State supervision of teaching—United States—Handbooks, manuals, etc. 2.
School districts—United States—Handbooks, manuals, etc. I. Title: State
takeover handbook. II. Title.
 LB2809.A2 G37 2003
 379.73—dc21

                                                              2002012990

∞™ The paper used in this publication meets the minimum requirements of
American National Standard for Information Sciences—Permanence of Paper
for Printed Library Materials, ANSI/NISO Z39.48-1992.
Manufactured in the United States of America.

CONTENTS

INTRODUCTION

State takeovers of local school districts unearth entrenched interests and face naysayers at every turn. These interventions are comparable to a ship's captain confronting a perilous storm. Angry parents, defiant politicians, and spurned school district administrators, stirred by state action perceived as racist and authoritarian, constitute the storm's elements. Energizing this storm is a growing awareness that schools are falling short in educating America's most disadvantaged children.

At least twenty-four state legislatures have authorized state takeovers. States, as captains of the educational ship, are choosing to steer straight into the eye of the storm. In the most recent illustration, the state of Pennsylvania decided to take over its Philadelphia school system. The state even moved to have Edison Schools, Inc., or another for-profit educational firm manage district operations and run some of its failing schools.[1]

This book offers lessons for these bold and possibly foolhardy states. My central thesis is that a command-and-control, authoritarian approach to takeovers is doomed to fail. This thesis is not new; indeed, many commentators oppose the state policy of takeovers on the ground that they are necessarily authoritarian. *Navigating Treacherous Waters*, though, charts a more realistic course. It assumes that state legislatures will continue endorsing takeovers as state policy, which begs an important question: how can takeovers be made effective?

Blending a decade of takeover accounts with lessons from law and business, *Navigating Treacherous Waters: A State Takeover Handbook* argues that those who execute takeovers should expect a mess. This mess is racial, legal, political, and bureaucratic, and I revisit these issues throughout the book.

Some, particularly those knowledgeable in the workings of institutions, will not be surprised to learn how messy takeovers can become. Yet I discovered shortly into my research that takeovers attracted little written, scholarly attention (beyond newspaper coverage), and even that attention sputtered out in the early 1990s. While many may have an intuitive understanding of the how-and-why of the takeover mess, there was little careful and analytical attention given to describing and sorting through the mess. In short, I write here what I expected to find when I started my research: a chief resource containing the bulk of existing takeover references and describing the experiences of state takeovers.

My less humble goal is to sift through the evidence from takeover experiences and to distill a series of best practices. This sifting does not pretend to survive the tests of reliability or validity; it does not compare school districts that have been taken over with those that have not. It instead travels a path described by the theorist Jane Jacobs in her work, *The Life and Death of Great American Cities*: "So in this book we shall start, if only in a small way, adventuring in the real world, ourselves. The way to get at what goes on . . . is to look closely, and with as little previous expectation as is possible, at the most ordinary scenes and events, and attempt to see what they mean and whether any threads or principle emerge among them."[2]

The most important principle emerging from takeover experiences is that better-executed state takeovers start with state actors who embrace collaboration and negotiation. The strategy of collaboration and negotiation is not better just because it leads to better outcomes. It exhausts every opportunity before an outright takeover happens, and avoiding the mess of an outright, authoritarian takeover is almost always preferable.

Along the way in arguing for collaboration and negotiation, I propose improvements in both the design and implementation of these interventions. Some proposals are fairly conventional. For example, I advocate for eliminating tenure rights in taken-over school districts. Others are more innovative. Takeover criteria, for instance, should include measures that states are sure they can improve. This outcome-based analysis results in criteria for facilities and finances that are currently absent from most takeover statutes.

Other proposals modify existing plans or practices. Observers have argued that the threat of a takeover is itself an effective spur to reform and should be the primary rationale behind takeovers. I press on and draft a structure based on deterrence. A recently passed Pennsylvania statute constructs an intervention advisory board composed of a school district's stakeholders. I advocate similar boards.

Chapter 1, "Takeover Basics," provides essential background, even for those familiar with takeovers. It walks through the process by which states take over local school districts, elaborates on the rationales supporting and opposing takeovers, and hits the recurring issues of race, law, and politics. Pro-takeover thinkers often analogize takeovers to bankruptcies.

Chapter 2, "Bankruptcy: The Default Model," is the first-of-its-kind attempt to take this analogy seriously by exploring the differences between bankruptcies and takeovers. While the analogy is ultimately disparaged, several insights are gained in the process. This chapter, too, represents where I think future takeover researchers can find a veritable gold mine by comparing state takeovers to the panoply of other interventions structures out there—for example, the International Monetary Fund in poor countries, military intervention in humanitarian situations, corporate takeovers, and so on.

Chapter 3, "An Innovative Framework," and chapter 4, "Executing Takeovers: A Last Resort," are this book's captain's deck and engine room. Both are sprinkled with experiences from takeovers and policy advocacy. The former constructs a takeover regime, which is the process by which a district is put on warning and, after failing to improve, taken over. The latter offers recommendations for actually implementing a state takeover. The list in chapter 4, "A Takeover Model: Policy and Practice," recaps all of these chapters' policy choices.

Navigating Treacherous Waters offers a bit for anyone who is touched by takeovers. Parents, community representatives, local educators, and administrators may see their own struggles and potential solutions. Students can explore, through the vehicle of takeovers, the competition between local control and equity. Academics will find why state takeovers are such an interesting subject and, from the ideas presented here, much to criticize, improve, or build. And most of all, state legislators and educational policy wonks will be armed with more information to make wiser choices.

NOTES

1. Karla Scoon Reid, "Community Groups Looking to Run Phila. Schools," *Ed. Wk.* (Feb. 6, 2002): 1.

2. Jane Jacobs, *The Death and Life of Great American Cities,* Vintage Books, 1992, 13.

1

TAKEOVER BASICS

Local school districts increasingly find themselves subject to state oversight.[1] Buoyed by the popular concept of accountability for students, schools, and school districts, state legislators and education officials have moved beyond oversight to outright state control of school districts. Referred to as a "state takeover," this is the ultimate tool in the accountability toolbox.

This chapter maps the basic geography of state takeovers. It describes how they happen, provides a historical explanation for their occurrence in the last decade, explores the rationales used to argue for and against these statutes, identifies recurring issues, and surveys the results of these state interventions.

THE PROCESS[2]

Takeovers happen when a state department of education finds that a district is either fiscally irresponsible or academically failing. Before 1989, fiscal irresponsibility triggered state control.[3] Since then, academic bankruptcy has been the justification for most takeovers.[4]

Two statutory paths can produce a takeover. In some cases, state legislatures target an individual school district, as in Compton, California;

Chicago, Illinois; Hartford, Connecticut; and Roosevelt, New York.[5] In others, takeover regimes commonly prescribe a series of stages that all school districts must move through before a takeover.[6]

Either way, an intervention trigger is pulled when a district fails to meet a minimum standard, which is usually a mixture of indices measured over several years. For example, Ohio measures eighteen indicators every year; sixteen of which are test-based. If a district fails on two-thirds of the eighteen indicators, it is designated as failing.[7] A failing district is put on warning, variously called *probation, academic deficiency,* or *under academic distress,* from which a number of fairly predictable events follow. First, a timer starts. If the district has not improved when time is up, a takeover (or strong intervention) results. Meanwhile, most states require that an improvement plan (frequently called a *corrective action plan*) is developed and implemented.[8] This improvement plan can be developed solely by state actors, or solely by local actors, or in coordination of the two.

State assistance at this point is usually technical (consultants, advisers, reports, and so on), and rarely financial.[9] Two exceptions deserve mention. Missouri allows for state aid but only when an audit suggests it.[10] A recent Pennsylvania statute takes a more liberal approach, requiring that school districts under threat of a takeover receive a base grant of $450,000 and additional grants of up to $75 per student.[11]

The school district is expected to improve while the timer ticks—for as few as sixty days in Louisiana[12] and up to three years in New Jersey[13]— or else face outright state takeover or further intervention. The medium for evaluation is usually a management team or auditor, while the ultimate decision rests in the hands of the state board or the state superintendent, often termed the chief state school officer (CSSO).

The standards for evaluation, though, vary among takeover statutes. For example, West Virginia asks only whether *any* progress has been made.[14] Ohio raises the bar a bit to require *satisfactory* progress.[15] More often, states ask whether the school district is failing to meet the plan's objectives or whether deadlines are being missed.

After a failure to meet the evaluation standard, the state board transfers responsibility for the district to the CSSO. As the district's caretaker, the CSSO faces many difficult decisions. Should the local school board and superintendent be suspended, disbanded, or moved into a purely advisory capacity? If, when, and how should employees be reviewed? Should extra funding be provided? What are appropriate timelines? Takeover legislation can affect these decisions, but more often than not, a statute's silence gives the CSSO discretion. Chapter 4 offers some answers to these questions and more.

Takeovers generally result in the replacement of the superintendent. The replacement, labeled a state administrator here, becomes the *de facto* manager of the school district. Almost all takeovers result in a reduction of the school board's powers: the board is either removed outright or relegated to advisory status. A forceful takeover results in a state administrator and a dissolved board. At its least forceful, a takeover results in a state administrator controlling only one area of district operations or having only veto powers.

This range of takeover options brings up an important distinction in takeover language: intervention versus takeover.[16] Drawing the line where one ends and the other begins is difficult but important. An intervention is likely to be perceived as helpful, thereby provoking little antagonism, where a takeover is inherently antagonizing. Replacing the board and superintendent is clearly a takeover. Mandating that a district develop and implement a corrective action plan is clearly an intervention. Disentangling the large in-between is more difficult. It is unclear what to call the relegation of a school board to advisory status, or the appointment of a state administrator who possesses only narrowly defined veto powers over the superintendent and board. Here are two working definitions that do not succeed in clarifying the murky middle, but at least provide a start: any involvement beyond mere assistance and short of direct state control is *intervention*. A *takeover* is day-to-day control of district operations and decision-making. I focus on the whole family of takeovers and some of their nearby interventionist kin.

SOME HISTORICAL EXPLANATIONS

The swell of takeovers in the 1990s was surprising because one set of takeover actors was mostly Republican, usually advocates of local control. Several historical and political factors compounded to explain this ironic result.[17]

The 1990s saw a fissure appear in the general reform trend of decentralization. In New York City, for example, a thirty-three-year revolt for community control, which started in 1966 and led to the creation of community school boards, ended after the New York State Legislature stripped these same boards of many of their hiring and budgetary powers.[18] In a further affront to decentralization, the legislature gave direct control of failing city schools to the city schools' chief.[19]

As state governments searched for the right balance between centralization and decentralization, they found that their share of the education bill increased. State legislatures bore an increasing proportion of the cost of public education relative to local governments. Increased share of the costs spurred increased responsibility that, in turn, spurred increased state regulation of school districts—for example, the California school code quadrupled in a generation.[20] Yet increased regulation did not result in pliable school districts acting at the state's bidding. Districts often ignored state directives because they understood that the state had no practical weapons.[21] Withholding funds—the traditional weapon to punish disobedient districts—was unpopular, so other measures, including takeovers, were considered.[22]

At the same time, education policy wonks began producing "effective schools" literature.[23] Policymakers believed that best practices derived from effective schools could help the worst-performing school districts succeed. Legislators, buoyed by an electorate more interested in education,[24] now had some policy to bring to bear on failing school districts.

Meanwhile, many Republican governors swept into office, such as Tommy Thompson in Wisconsin, New Jersey's Thomas Kean, Pete Wilson of California, and Michigan's John Engler. These governors and many like-minded legislators valued local control but held a deep distrust for the public-education bureaucracy.[25] Combine a clamoring electorate, a fissure in the decentralization movement, educational theorists positing best practices for all schools, and an initial distrust of public bureaucracies, and the pot boiled for sure.

RATIONALES

The central philosophical puzzle of school takeovers is which principle should triumph: local control or equal opportunity. Local control—

vouched in legal principle, held dear by parents, teachers, and local administrators, and praised by politicians on the right and left—is a deeply cherished American principle. But failing school districts, typically urban and predominantly minority,[26] fail the test of another principle: equal opportunity. A journalist expressed this best. Sure, state control is punitive for local school boards, principals, and teachers: "They had it coming. Students in taken-over schools aren't being punished; they're getting a genuine education, and hence a chance in life, that they would otherwise be denied."[27]

The pro-takeover argument is two-pronged. First, these statutes spur poorly performing school districts to improve through deterrence alone. The threat of takeover can be generally directed to all poorly performing districts or specifically to a single district. Second, state intervention or outright takeover can improve district performance by implementing good management and leadership, and eliminating corruption and patronage.

Deterrence

Taking over failing schools sends a message to school boards of failing school districts. Though directed at one school district, the threat of a takeover puts *all* failing or near-failing schools on notice that they might be next. New York Governor George Pataki put it plainly while discussing a takeover of the Roosevelt school district, "If this works, I think districts that are failing would be at a significantly greater risk of losing control."[28] The eighty school districts in New York state undergoing registration review presumably understood the governor's message.

A threat can achieve its desired effect.[29] For example, the Penns-Grove Carney Point school district had moved through New Jersey's takeover regime and was one step from takeover. The district superintendent described the shame: "No one likes to be in that category because it connotes that you are not fulfilling your obligation educationally for children."[30] The state cited the district for two major problems: lack of written curriculum and substandard facilities.[31] The superintendent described how this stigma turned into action:

[Being one step from takeover] did, however, get the district to examine itself, take a look at things educationally and work for programs for the children. Not that the district didn't want these programs and improvements before, but we have a tendency to put on the back burner some things that could be done today. [It] forced us to roll up our sleeves and do what we had to do.[32]

As a result, the district wrote the curriculum and passed a bond to improve facilities.[33]

Sometimes the threat of a takeover is targeted at a specific school district outside of a formal takeover regime. For example, Wisconsin Governor Tommy Thompson warned that, unless academics improved, their state's biggest school district faced imminent takeover: "It's time for MPS [Milwaukee Public Schools] to stand and deliver or step aside."[34] He pointed to four rates that required improvement: dropout, attendance, graduation, and third-grade reading scores.[35]

To have a meaningful deterrent effect, a statute's threat must be genuine; the state must have the political will to exercise the takeover option. The success or failure of any individual takeover becomes only secondarily important. By demonstrating willingness to take over a school district, even a failed takeover may spur improvement in other poorly performing districts, and the deterrent rationale is preserved. For example, while the state intervention in Detroit, Michigan, might or might not result in district improvement, a state threat to a nearby school district prompted quick action. The school board president of Inkster, Michigan, justified the board's decision to delegate district management to a private education management company: "The route we're looking at is a better route than having the state takeover."[36]

Improvement

Takeover proponents use three arguments to show that state involvement can lead to improvement. First, the state cannot perform worse than the current administration. Second, state intervention improves management and leadership. Third, the state roots out corruption and patronage.

Many important players, particularly governors, believe that district administration cannot get worse.[37] Takeovers are usually preceded by several audits and reports that describe bad physical conditions, poor administration, and little focus on academic achievement. One audit of a Kentucky school system (later taken over) found filthy restrooms, a homebound program being used as a dumping ground for troubled kids, and a complete lack of administrative procedures and financial controls.[38] In Newark, New Jersey, one state official described how top administrators had expense accounts at thirty-two restaurants.[39]

These dire conditions present an opportunity to do better, especially in relation to school management and leadership. Sometimes one bad actor is at the center of mismanagement and lack of leadership. A Richmond, California, superintendent led the district into a deficit of more than $30 million.[40] A state official called the superintendent a "financial charlatan;"[41] indeed, later research revealed a pattern of mismanagement, verging on fraud and corruption, that followed the superintendent from districts in New Jersey, Texas, and Ohio.[42]

Other times, it is a matter of focusing on better leadership and management. This usually begins with replacing the district superintendent and removing power from the school board. As a former New Jersey CSSO vividly explained, "You have to absolutely, absolutely, get rid of the people who brought you the problem. If a person has brought you pestilence and famine, you don't say, 'Gee I'd like to work with you for another two or three years.'"[43] States can replace these figures with local personnel, or more typically, with state officers or handpicked experts. The next step is usually an intensive review of top administrative personnel, including school principals, that is often followed by firings.

Yet firings and staff review are not prerequisites for better management and leadership. Sometimes it is as simple as resolving an administrative blunder. In Logan County, West Virginia, a third of the teachers didn't have proper certification because the teachers' applications had been sitting in a box underneath the personnel director's desk. All that needed to be done was to forward these applications to the state certification board.[44]

Rooting out patronage and corruption is an important argument for better district management. School districts fail, the argument goes, when they care more about services for adults than about kids.[45] Since takeover targets care typically poor communities, where school districts are often the largest employers in the communities,[46] the story of schools as patronage machines is nowhere truer than here.[47]

In Newark, the school budget of more than $500 million raised the question of corruption and patronage. Its annual per-pupil expenditure was nearly $10,000, on par with the richest suburban school districts.[48] Meanwhile, only four eighth-grade teachers in the entire system were qualified to teach Algebra I.[49] Per-pupil expenditure on the lunch program was $4 compared with a $2 average across the state."[50] Patronage is the likely explanation for these disparities, particularly since the school board, in a highly irregular practice, voted on every employee hired.[51] Sometimes school board members themselves prove corrupt. In Compton, California, two school board members were charged with (and one was convicted of) fraud.[52]

It is hard to conclude whether a state intervention and/or takeover roots out corruption. As discussed later in this chapter, state involvement reduces district costs, which by implication suggests an effect on corruption. The firing of high-level administrators and personnel is another indication of anticorruption success.

The Powerless State

While the pro-takeover argument depends in large part on the sorry state of a failing school district's affairs, anti-takeover arguments discount the state's ability to do any better. The following arguments are far fewer in number than the pro-takeover arguments. Yet, if true or even mostly true, they are fatal blows to the pro-takeover arguments. Summarized by the theory of institutional choice, the arguments wonder why a new authority is any more capable of achieving desired results than the old one. Put differently, what does the alternative decision maker—the state—offer beyond the current decision maker—the local school district?[53] This shift in focus produces two anti-takeover arguments. First, the wisdom to solve educational problems resides in the locality. Detroit Mayor Dennis Archer explained his preference for local wisdom: "Whatever the problems in the Detroit public schools—and there are problems—we have not reached the point where Lansing can educate Detroit children better than Detroiters."[54]

Second, environmental factors will thwart attempts to turn around a failing school district. Since a change in district leadership will not affect students' poverty, broken families, or low self-esteem, state intervention is doomed to fail. If the state cannot fix these things, the president of the Newark school board argued, it should stay out of district affairs. A Compton board president, arguing to a state assemblyman who advocated a state takeover, pointed out that the school board had two members who were attorneys and three who had masters' degrees.[55] Expertise, the president argued, surely is not the problem.[56] Further, he suggested, if the assemblyman wanted improvement:

> [Then] work on legislation to provide jobs to reduce unemployment of our youths after they graduate. You introduce and support legislation that would make college education affordable for students of our district. I would love to see you address the problem of neglected children and drug babies with the same enthusiasm that you address the problems of this district.[57]

An academic might read a more sinister purpose into the state's disregard of environmental factors: takeovers not taking into account the systemic problems facing a school district are really "symbolic gestures" intended to silence those clamoring for real reform.[58]

RECURRING ISSUES

Interventions and/or takeovers are not nearly as simple as passing a law, deciding to whom it applies, and proceeding. A journalist described the complications: "When state administrators have tried to elbow out local officials and run a failing district themselves, improvements have come at the heavy cost of lawsuits, bitter media battles, and confused and angry teachers and parents."[59] The three most important takeover complications are race, politics, and law. Each recalls arguments from the previous section.

Race

Race is important to both opponents and supporters of takeovers. The race-based, anti-takeover argument is that takeovers are an oppressive tactic of nonminority outsiders, and that, by intervening, the state diminishes minority political power.[60] One Compton activist and ex-school board member characterized the movement from a bumbling local administration to a state-led one, "We went from knuckleheads to skinheads. We're paying [the state administrator] to denigrate and hate us."[61] Sometimes takeover leaders are seen as allies of "white corporate executives and politicians,"[62] and minority state administrators have done little to lessen these charges or the underlying racial tensions.

Race-based arguments are less often used to support or urge a takeover. A local African American politician, responding to the governor's veto of a Compton takeover, said:

> I am utterly disgusted and disappointed with the veto because no one seems to care that 28,000 little poor, black and Hispanic children are not receiving even a minimal education. If these were Anglo kids, these educational conditions would not be tolerated.[63]

In considering the racial implications of a district takeover, a Detroit minister put it differently: "We assert that the only race that matters is the race that succeeds in properly educating our children before another generation is lost."[64] This point of view, reversing the more traditional race argument against takeovers, suggests that state inaction shows a disregard for minority children suffering from substandard academic services.[65]

Law

Takeovers are often followed by court challenges that, in turn, lead to implementation problems. There are three types of court challenges.[66] The first is a byproduct of anti-takeover, race-based arguments. Since taken-over school districts are often in minority communities, the consequent reduction (or elimination) of an elected school board's power results in minority disenfranchisement and exposes a takeover to a voting-rights challenge.[67] This challenge has reached the U.S. Supreme Court, but for technical reasons, the court declined to rule, which had the effect of leaving state takeover laws intact.[68] Second, a due-process challenge goes to a board member's rights in his or her job.[69] Third, an equal protection challenge goes to the right of a school district to be treated fairly in relation to other districts.[70]

These challenges are rarely successful,[71] but they leave school district personnel and state actors in limbo about who will be where and for how long. Moreover, they cost money. The school board in Jersey City, New Jersey, spent $1.4 million in defending against a state takeover.[72] In Letcher County, Kentucky, parties returned to court several times to enforce a consent decree.[73] In Illinois, an appeal took three years before the state could supervise educational as well as financial matters.[74] Compton,[75] Newark,[76] and Detroit[77] also faced court challenges.

In two highly unusual examples, courts have *ordered* the state to take over local school districts. Several years ago, an Ohio court found the Cleveland system in a state of crisis and ordered a takeover.[78] A district in California experienced a similar takeover, although it was based on financial mismanagement.[79] While exceptional, if proponents of an educational adequacy standard succeed, these cases may become common.

Politics

The politics of local control pits local politicians against politicians from state capitals, local education administrators against state education administrators, and state policymakers against local activists. This struggle has been conducted on two geographical fronts: only urban and rural school districts have faced the takeover threat.[80]

Takeovers involve politics in two ways. First, takeover legislation generates turf battles between political parties. On the one hand, Democratic mayors or city councils rule many of the usual targets of takeovers—urban areas. Governors, on the other hand, recently have more often been Republican. For example, a former New Jersey local superintendent described the Jersey City takeover as a "simple matter of Trenton Republicans with a vendetta against Jersey City and Hudson County Democrats."[81] Also, changes in governors or CSSOs (elected in some states, appointed by a governor or a state board of education in others) can mean takeovers that change staff and values midstream.[82]

Second, local officials and activists create an especially political atmosphere. One commentator put it this way, "The saga of the Jersey City Public Schools most probably has its roots in the Jersey City tradition of mixing politics and education, which dates back at least 70 years to the tenure of mayor and political boss Frank Hague."[83] Less philo-sophic but no less real, local school board meetings can produce fire-works. In Newark, New Jersey, community members greeted the state administrator Beverly Hall at a board meeting with chants of "Hall, you liar, gonna set your butt on fire!"[84]

RESULTS

Although takeover results offer little to resolve the arguments under-lying state takeovers, they provide a valuable perspective for inter-preting takeover statutes and experiences. Financial management, most observers agree, is the one area where state takeovers have suc-ceeded.[85] The worse the situation, the more corruption prior to takeover, the more success the takeover demonstrates.[86] In Newark, New Jersey, the state reorganized the district and freed up $26 million for instruction,[87] while the $4 billion projected deficit for Chicago schools was eliminated.[88]

However, most observers find no academic gains from takeovers.[89] If gains are possible, some argue, they show only after a decade of in-volvement.[90] Only three districts are exceptions to this rule. First, a state takeover in Logan County, West Virginia, left behind higher test scores and lower dropout rates.[91] Second, after five years of a takeover, schools' reading scores in Compton, California, have risen for three successive years.[92] Third, students in Chicago schools have higher scores on tests, including college entrance exams.[93]

The failure of the majority of takeovers to increase academic achieve-ment does not end the debate. Academic increases tend to show only af-ter several years, and even if they do not show, a state intervention may build a school district's capacity to affect academic achievement. Capac-ity building can be financial, managerial, intellectual, or political,[94] and results in long-term, positive outcomes.[95] Examples are professional de-velopment, district reorganization, private-public partnerships, or ex-panded teacher recruitment.

A capacity-building state intervention occurred in Chelsea, Massa-chusetts. With the approval of the Massachusetts legislature, local offi-cials and Boston University agreed to let the university run the district's operations.[96] The city's elected school committee can overrule, with a two-thirds majority, the university team on policy issues and can terminate the relationship with a simple majority.[97] A legislative report found that this relationship has resulted in a lower dropout rate and competitive teacher salaries.[98] Recently, city officials decided to extend the management agreement for another five years.[99] However, even with these successes, no academic improvement has been shown.

The next chapter drifts away from the forces affecting takeovers and the day-to-day anecdotes common to them. It drifts up to consider the takeover concept as viewed through the lens of bankruptcy.

NOTES

1. Joan McRobbie, "Can State Intervention Spur Academic Turnaround," *West Ed Hot Topic 1998,* at web.WestEd.org/online_pubs/state_intervention /SI.html (accessed April 6, 2002).

2. See Todd Zierbarth, *State Takeovers and Reconstitutions,* Education Commission of the States, rev. 2001, for an overview of takeover statutes and a compilation of legal citations to takeover statutes.

3. See Richard Hunter and Jeff Swann, "School Takeovers and Enhanced Answerability," *Educ. & Urb. Soc'y* 31 (1999): 238, 243 (noting takeovers based on financial problems in New Jersey, Ohio, and California).

4. David Berman, "Takeovers of Local Government: An Overview and Evaluation of State Policies," *Publius* (Summer 1995): 56.

5. Compton, Calif.: Karen Diegmueller, "Academic Deficiencies Force Takeover of California School District," *Ed. Wk.* (Sep. 16, 1992): 21; Chicago, Ill.: Ron Stodghill, "Mayors Rule the Schools," *Time* (Apr. 12, 1999) at 74; Hartford, Conn.: Jeff Archer, "Connecticut Bill to Seize Hartford Schools Passes," *Ed. Wk.* (Apr. 23, 1997): 1; Roosevelt, N.Y.: David Bauder, "Pataki Signs Bill Granting School District Takeover," *Buff. News* (Jul. 20, 1995): A6.

6. See David Mayrowetz and James Pennell, "A Naturalistic Inquiry of Envisioned Worlds: Conceptualizing and Classifying State Intervention Laws," *Amer. Educ. Ass'n Res. Paper* 9–13 (1997).

7. Oh St. §3302.2

8. One analyst counted seventeen laws that mandated twenty-two corrective action plans. David Mayrowetz and James Pennell, "A Naturalistic Inquiry of Envisioned Worlds: Conceptualizing and Classifying State Intervention Laws," *Amer. Educ. Ass'n Res. Paper* 11 (1997).

9. American Federation of Teachers, "Survey of State Legislation on School Takeovers," *Educ. Issues Pol'y Brief,* Oct. 1997, at www.aft.org//Edissues /policybriefs/download/policyone.pdf (accessed April 6, 2002).

10. MO St. §160.538

11. 24 P.S. §17-1709(B).

12. LA R.S. §391.10

13. NJ ST §18A: 7A(14)-(15.1)

14. WV ST §18(2)(e)(5)(k)(3)

15. OH Admin. Code §3301-15-05(F)(3)

16. See Charles Mahtesian, "Whose Schools?" *Governing Mag.,* (Sep. 1997): 34–38.

17. Hypocritical may be a more apt descriptor. See Alan Ehrendalt, "Powerless Pipsqueaks and the Myth of Local Control," *Governing Mag.* (Jun. 1999) (arguing that local control proponents use the principle only as a means to a political end).

18. See Lydia Segal, "The Pitfalls of Political Decentralization and Proposals for Reform: The Case of New York City Public Schools," *Pub. Ad. Rev.* 57 (1997): 141. See also Kenneth K. Wong, Robert Dreeben, Laurence E. Lynn Jr., and Gail L. Sunderman, "Integrated Governance as a Reform Strategy in the Chicago Public Schools," *Laboratory Spotlight on Student Success* No. 205 (1997) (noting a decentralization swing in the mid-1990s Chicago schools system).

19. Segal, "Pitfalls."

20. David Kirp and Cyrus Driver, "The Aspirations of Systemic Reform Meet the Realities of Localism," *Ed. Admin. Q.* 31 (1995): 589, 593.

21. Kirp and Driver, "Aspirations," 589.

22. Susan Fuhrman and Richard Elmore, "Takeover and Deregulation: Working Models of New State and Local Regulatory Relationships," *Cons. for Pol'y Res. in Educ. Res. Rep.* 4 (1992).

23. Thomas Gusky, "Policy Issues and Options When States Take over Local School Districts," *Int'l J. of Educ. Reform* 2 (1992): 68, 68–69.

24. Gusky, "Policy Issues," 69.

25. William Clune, "Institutional Choice as a Theoretical Framework for Research on Educational Policy," *Educ. Eval. and Pol'y Analysis* 9 (1987): 117, 120.

26. See Linda Wertheimer, "School District Takeovers Get Mixed Grades," *Dal. Morn. News* (Mar. 14, 1999): A37.

27. Nicholas Lehman, "'Ready, READ!' A new solution to the problem of failing schools is emerging," *Atl. Mnthly* (Nov. 1998): 92–104.

28. See David Bauder, "Pataki Signs Bill Granting School District Takeover," *Buff. News* (Jul. 20, 1995): A6.

29. In Arkansas, a takeover law threatened twenty-five school districts. A superintendent described the reaction to a finding of academic distress: "There was definitely a stigma attached to it, but that's part of it. It's kind of a wake-up call for us." David Hoff, "Takeovers Threatened, 25 Arkansas Districts Address Deficiencies," *Ed. Wk.* (Oct. 2, 1996): 17. In the late 1980s, a Kentucky deficiency program was credited with encouraging low-achieving districts to reach and maintain minimum standards, primarily through deterrent effects. According to a state staff person, the threat of intervention caused twenty-three school districts to get out of substandard status by increasing attendance and decreasing dropouts. Patricia Fry et al., "Kentucky's Program for Educationally Deficient School Districts: A Case Study," *Cons. for Pol'y Res. in Educ. Res. Reports* 14 (1992). See also Wertheimer, "School District Takeovers," A37 (citing Union City, N.J.'s, replacement of a superintendent after nearby districts taken over).

30. Mary Skelly, "A New Jersey Success Story," *Sch. and College* 28 (1989): 11.

31. Skelly, "Success Story," 11.

32. Skelly, "Success Story," 11.

33. Skelly, "Success Story," 11.

34. Beth Reinhard, "Thompson Threatens a Takeover for Milwaukee," *Ed. Wk.* (Jan. 28, 1998): 14.

35. Reinhard, "Thompson Threatens a Takeover."

36. "Inkster Turns to Private Firm to Manage Schools," *Mich. Educ. Rep.,* May 12, 2000, at www.educationreport.org/pubs/mer/article.asp?ID=2858 (accessed July 11, 2002).

37. See e.g., David Bauder, "Pataki Signs Bill Granting School District Takeover," *Buff. News* (Jul. 20, 1995): A6. (Governor of New York: "I believe in local control," but he thought it evident there was no control at all in Roosevelt Union Free School District.); Richard Burr, "State Takeovers Display Mixed Education Results," *Det. News* (Feb. 9, 1997): B5. (Governor of Michigan: "We cannot sit by and ignore the problems in the name of local control. . . . So many of these systems have made it impossible to do worse.").

38. Mark Schaver, "Letcher School Board to Let State Take over Schools," *Courier J.* (1994): B1.

39. Laura Litvan, "States Try to Rescue Schools," *Investor's Bus. Daily* (Feb. 17, 1998): A1.

40. Charles Hardy and Scott Winokur, "Long Trail of Misconduct: Marks' Leadership of Richmond Schools Continued His Pattern of Misspending," *San Fran. Chron.* (May 26, 1991): A1.

41. Diane Curtis, "Richmond School Board Rebuked," *San Fran. Chron.* (Jul. 18, 1991): A15.

42. Hardy and Winokur, "Long Trail of Misconduct," A1.

43. Mahtesian, "Whose Schools?" 34–38.

44. David Hoff, "W. Va. Leaves District Better Than It Found It," *Ed. Wk.* (Sep. 18, 1996): 17.

45. Beverly Hall, "State Intervention in the Newark Public Schools," *Instit. for Educ. and Soc. Pol'y Occasional Paper* 3 (1998). A legislator described the effects of hiring based on patronage: "Because superintendents and locally elected boards dispense jobs, we get a deficient system perpetuating a deficient system. Employees have political skills but not necessarily educational skills." Fry et al., "Kentucky's Program for Educationally Deficient School Districts."

46. The district in Floyd County, Ky., was the largest employer. Fry et al., "Kentucky's Program for Educationally Deficient School Districts." The school district in Newark, N.J., was the second largest employer. Hall, "State Intervention in the Newark Public Schools."

47. For example, a study of New York City public schools detailed a patronage system where board members were called "godfathers" and "godmothers" because of their ability to provide jobs for family members and friends or in exchange for sexual favors, bribes, or political contributions. The receivers of patronage were called "pieces;" principals were "plum pieces" because of their access to voting parents. See Lydia Segal, "The Pitfalls of Political Decentralization and Proposals for Reform: The Case of New York City Public Schools," *Pub. Adm. Rev.* 57 (1997): 141.

48. Hall, "State Intervention in the Newark Public Schools," 2.

49. Hall, "State Intervention in the Newark Public Schools," 2.

50. Hall, "State Intervention in the Newark Public Schools," 2.

51. Hall, "State Intervention in the Newark Public Schools," 3.

52. Heather Finnegan and Scott Rivera, *School Takeover: A Case Study in Compton, Calif.,* Eyebrow Films (1999).

53. See William Clune, "Institutional Choice as a Theoretical Framework for Research on Educational Policy," *Ed. Eval. and Pol'y Analysis* 9 (1987): 117–18. An analogous concept, systems changing, uses cost-benefit language. The state delivers the benefit of its new authority but costs because of the absence of local authority. This theory predicts a defensive local response with a potential for positive action. See Lorraine McDonnell and Richard Elmore, "Getting the Job Done: Alternative Policy Instruments," *Ed. Eval. and Pol'y Analysis* 9 (1987): 133.

54. Caroline Hendrie, "Plan to Allow Mich. School Takeover Hailed," *Ed. Wk.* (Feb. 12, 1997): 15.

55. Howard Blume, "Legislator Defends Proposal for School District Takeover," *L.A. Times* (Sep. 10, 1992): 1.

56. Blume, "Legislator Defends Proposal," 1.

57. Blume, "Legislator Defends Proposal," 1.

58. Richard Hunter and Jeff Swann, "School Takeovers and Enhanced Answerability," *Educ. & Urb. Soc'y* 31 (1999): 238, 250.

59. Caroline Hendrie, "Ill Will Comes with Territory in Takeovers," *Ed. Wk.* (Jun. 12, 1996): 1.

60. See, e.g., Glenn Rice, "African American Leaders Speak Out against School District Takeover," *Kan. City Star* (Mar. 22, 2001): B1.

61. Howard Blume, "2nd Loan Sought for Compton School District Schools," *L.A. Times*, B3.

62. Beth Reinhard, "Mayor to Get School Control in Cleveland," *Ed. Wk.* (Jul. 9, 1992): 1, 29.

63. Howard Blume, "Compton Schools Face Twin Crises," *L.A. Times* (Oct. 2, 1992): B1.

64. Tracy Van Moorlehem, "School Takeover Bid Gets Endorsements," *Det. Free Press* (Feb. 27, 1999): A8.

65. Demographic shifts may shape the race question differently in the coming decade. While inner cities boast larger proportions of Latinos, the makeup of city governance largely remains African American. One commentator termed the trend *The Second Apartheid*. Mike Davis, "The Sky Falls on Compton: Death and Taxes," *Nation* (Sep. 19, 1994): 271. This trend has played itself out in school district politics. After a search for school board candidates, the Compton school board chose to overlook a top-rated Latino applicant, choosing instead an African American who had a felony conviction for selling false traffic-school diplomas. A state senator called the decision "myopic and racist." Psyche Pascual, "Compton Murray Calls Decision by School Board Racist," *L.A. Times,* (Dec. 1, 1994): 8. See also Kerry White, "Silber and Chelsea: A Lasting Legacy," *Ed. Wk.* (Nov. 5, 1997): 31. (Less severe charges of ignoring or being insensitive to Latinos have been leveled at the university-run district in Chelsea, Mass.)

66. A March 2001 court challenge by the city of Newark charged the state, in control of the district since 1995, with financial mismanagement. This lawsuit is the first of its kind. Karla Scoon Reid, "Newark Sues State District Over Losses," *Ed. Wk.* (Feb. 14, 2001): 1, 18.

67. See Beth Reinhard, "Racial Issues Cloud State Takeovers," *Ed. Wk.* (Jan. 14, 1998): 1. Texas v. United States, 523 U.S. 296 (1998); Victoria Salzmann, "State of Texas v. United States: Voting Rights and Texas's Educational Standards," *Baylor Law Review* 51 (Winter 1999): 191; Spivey v. Ohio, 999 F. Supp. 987 (N. D. Ohio 1988).

68. See Texas, supra note 70.

69. See East St. Louis Federation of Teachers v. East St. Louis Sch. District, 178 Ill. 2d 399 (1997) (finding no due process or equal protection violations).

70. See East St. Louis Federation of Teachers v. East St. Louis Sch. District.

71. Legal analysts have supported the court's noninvolvement in takeovers: Aaron Saiger, "Note: Disestablishing Local School Districts as a Remedy for Educational Inadequacy," *Colum. L. Rev.* 99 (1999): 1830; Ronald Hyman, "State-Operated Local School Districts in New Jersey," *Ed. Law Rep.* 96 (1995): 915; F. Clinton Broden, "Litigating State Constitutional Rights to an Adequate Education and the Remedy of State-Operated School Districts," *Rutgers L. Rev.* 42 (1990): 779.

72. Michael Rettig, "Policy Adaptation and Change: The Case of the State Takeover of Jersey City Public Schools," *Amer. Educ. Res. Ass'n paper* 6 (1992).

73. "Letcher Schools Fighting State Again," *Courier J.,* Louisville, Ky. (Aug. 22, 1996): B1.

74. See Laura Litvan, "States Try to Rescue Schools," A1.

75. "California Sued for Providing Inadequate Education in Poor School District," American Civil Liberties Union press release, July 7, 1997, at www.aclu.org/news/n071097b.html (accessed Apr. 6, 2002).

76. Mahtesian, "Whose Schools?" 34–38.

77. Mario Ortiz, "Takeover Challenge Announced," *Det. Free Press* (Apr. 7, 1999): B8.

78. See Reinhard, "Racial Issues Cloud State Takeovers," 18.

79. See Butt v. California, 4 Cal. 4th 668, 842 P. 2d 1240 (1992).

80. The too-easy explanation argues that suburban districts perform well academically, thereby avoiding the state's attention. However, because performance probably resembles a bell curve distribution, a set of suburban districts must perform poorly relative to other suburban districts. These districts may not face the takeover threat because they lack the sensationalistic corruption and patronage existing in many urban and rural districts. But corruption and patronage are discovered in audits and reports after state intervention and usually prior to takeover. It seems reasonable to predict that, after state intervention in a poorly performing suburban district, such bad acts may be found.

81. Margaret Dolan, "State Takeover of a Local School District in New Jersey: A Case Study," *Cons. for Pol'y Res. in Educ. Res. Report Series TC-008* 10 (1992).

82. See Mahtesian, "Whose Schools?" 34–38.

83. Rettig, "Policy Adaptation and Change," 4.

84. See Mahtesian, "Whose Schools?" 34–38.

85. See generally Litvan, "States Try to Rescue Schools," A1; Todd Ziebarth, "State Takeovers and Reconstitutions Policy Brief," *Ed. Comm. of the States* (1998); Hendrie, "Ill Will Comes with Territory," 1.

86. Takeovers often result in a dramatic reduction in superintendent and board members' perks. In Newark, N.J., the state cut perks after finding out

that top administrators had expense accounts at thirty-two restaurants and attended conferences in Hawaii. Litvan, "States Try to Rescue Schools," A1. After the state ceded power, Detroit's mayor deprived board members of stipends, corporate credit cards, cell phones, and pagers. Stodghill, "Mayors Rule the Schools," 74.

87. Litvan, "States Try to Rescue Schools," A1.

88. Burr, "State Takeovers Display Mixed Education Results," B5.

89. See Ziebarth, "State Takeovers and Reconstitutions Policy Brief;" Hendrie, "Ill Will Comes with Territory in Takeovers," 1.

90. White, "Silber and Chelsea: A Lasting Legacy," 31.

91. Hoff, "W. Va. Leaves District Better Than It Found It," 17.

92. "CUSD Students Score New Highs in CAT/5," press release from Compton Unified School District at www.compton.k12.ca.us/PR/PR05162000.htm (accessed Jul. 14, 2002).

93. Burr, "State Takeovers Display Mixed Education Results," B5.

94. See McDonnell and Elmore, "Getting the Job Done: Alternative Policy Instruments," 133.

95. See generally Paul Hill, "Helping Hands," Brookings Rev. 18 (Jul. 1, 2000): 3.

96. White, "Silber and Chelsea: A Lasting Legacy," 31.

97. White, "Silber and Chelsea: A Lasting Legacy," 31.

98. White, "Silber and Chelsea: A Lasting Legacy," 31.

99. White, "Silber and Chelsea: A Lasting Legacy," 31.

2

BANKRUPTCY: THE DEFAULT MODEL

A state takeover follows a familiar pattern: crisis and intervention. The *crisis* is a district's failure, and the *intervention* is state involvement. The difficulty of crisis and intervention should not be underestimated. Many undoubtedly chalk up a state's failure to improve academic achievement in a taken-over district as just another example of the public school system's failure. This chapter, using the bankruptcy model, shows that the private sector, too, is unfit to deal with crisis and intervention, at least in reference to bankrupt companies. One essayist captured the difficulty of crisis and intervention in one of the United State's most respected professions: "Good doctors can go bad, and when they do the medical profession is almost entirely unequipped to do anything about it."[1]

Bankruptcy is one model of crisis and intervention, and it happens to be the default model in takeover discourse.[2] Other models deserve scrutiny, which, through comparison with takeovers, will engender alternative courses of action. Some examples are hostile corporate takeovers, a baseball commissioner's interference with franchises, professional crisis management including so-called corporate turnaround artists, courts' treatment of abused or neglected children, and international military and humanitarian interventions.

Let's consider the broad-brush analogy of bankruptcy and takeovers. A corporation is made up of its management and staff, provides a product to its customers, and is accountable to its stockholders through the company's board of directors. Meanwhile, it has a legal obligation to pay off its creditors. A bankruptcy court, as an organ of the state, enters to remedy the discrepancy between corporate funds and credit obligations, partly by guaranteeing future corporate revenue to creditors, and partly by reorganizing the debt. A district is comparably composed of administration and staff, provides a product to its students, and is accountable to the community through the elected school board. Under a takeover regime, it is obliged to meet a state-set minimum performance standard. The state enters to remedy a failure to meet this standard, partly by involving itself in district operations and management, and partly by affecting district governance.

While a good start for exploring crisis and intervention, the bankruptcy comparison can be made carelessly. The executive director of the National School Boards Association summed up the carelessness:

> A referee in bankruptcy sorts out creditors' claims, presses debtors for payment, and conserves assets according to precise, universally understood rules with the irrefutably clear standard of the dollar. The referee does not operate the business. . . . [With takeovers:] What rules will be applied? And against what standards will its work be measured. . . . And where does a citizen take an appeal?[3]

This analysis correctly argues that takeovers cannot have the same "irrefutable" standard as bankruptcies and that states "operate" school districts during takeovers, as opposed to just sorting out claims. Deeper analysis, though, suggests a more nuanced comparison of the two model's purpose, criteria, and process.

THE PURPOSE

The executive director's analysis errs in which *kind* of bankruptcy to which to compare state takeovers. Chapter seven bankruptcies—the executive director's focus—aim to liquidate a bankrupt individual's assets,

meaning the assets are sold off to pay the bankrupt individual's creditors.[4] Analogized to takeovers, liquidation means either district annexation by an adjoining school district or simple dissolution, where the district ceases to exist and its students go to surrounding districts.[5] Neither
option, however, has been tried.

Chapter eleven bankruptcy is the more apt comparison. The purpose
of chapter eleven bankruptcy (applied to corporations rather than indi-
viduals) is to rehabilitate the bankrupt.[6] Creditors depend on a debtor's
future earnings, rather than a liquidation of the debtor's current posses-
sions.[7] Likewise, the purpose of a state takeover statute is to enable or
compel a school district to properly discharge its duty to educate children. The rest of this section considers only the comparison to chapter
eleven bankruptcies.

THE CRITERIA

A corporation is eligible for bankruptcy when its funds cannot cover its
credit obligations. This standard provides little guidance for state
takeovers. Bankruptcy criteria miss a crucial element present in
takeover statutes: conflict. Measuring pupil achievement requires entering a minefield of equity and pedagogical concerns. At the same time,
while bankruptcy parties have freely entered into an earlier contract,
state–district relations are defined by unilateral state action, not by contract or consent. A state legislature imposes a takeover structure, and
the state department of education, as its agent, executes it.

Bankruptcy criteria, which, akin to takeover criteria, expanded in the
last decade,[8] predict a troubling trend for takeovers. Some corporate
managers regard bankruptcies as tools for corporate reorganization, in
part because of lessened stigma around bankruptcy.[9] Will state
takeovers become a fairly usual tool for school district improvement? In
early 2001, one school district requested state intervention and another
requested state control to be extended for several years.[10] While only
anecdotal evidence, this trend suggests reduced stigma around
takeovers. If so, the deterrent rationale for state takeovers is seriously
undercut. In addition, the states' readiness and willingness to meet increased demand is in question.

THE PROCESS

Bankruptcies follow a consistent pattern: a debtor is found bankrupt, business operations continue, a rehabilitation plan is formulated, creditors and the court revise and accept the plan, and payments begin.[11] This process reflects the basics of early state intervention, differing only in what an improvement plan is called—the rehabilitation plan.

Underlying this basic similarity are five important contrasts to takeover processes. Two are structural, while the last three are relevant to what happens *later* in state intervention. The structure of bankruptcy differs from state takeovers in the role of negotiation and in the formation of creditors' committees. Bankruptcies usually involve negotiation while takeovers rarely do. A bankruptcy rehabilitation plan is proposed by the debtor, negotiated between the debtor and creditors, and finally approved by creditors and then the bankruptcy judge.[12] Also, negotiation is the chief mode for prebankruptcy affairs, too. Failing firms more often than not negotiate terms with creditors rather than undergo the bankruptcy process.[13] Yet, starting with a school district's development of an improvement plan and ending with an outright state takeover, negotiation is likely absent.[14]

Creditors' committees, often used in chapter eleven bankruptcy proceedings, do not have an existing analogy in state takeovers. Composed ordinarily of the seven largest creditors willing to serve, a creditors' committee consults on administrative matters, participates in formulating the rehabilitation plan, and makes recommendations to accept or reject the plan.[15] A bankruptcy expert analyzed the implementation problem posed by creditors' committees:

> [A]dditional committees should be the norm. . . . But multiplying the number of players in the game costs money, sometimes lots of money and may increase the complexity of the reorganization. Appointment of additional committees might diminish the power of the judge, or other parties, to control the reorganization procedure. The judge may already find himself astride an unruly horse and may not relish the thought of yet another actor to spook his mount.[16]

The judge's problem with a spooked or unruly horse aptly describes the state's problem in a school district's takeover—indeed, the metaphor returns in chapter 4. The difference, however, is that takeovers *consistently* result in a spooked horse because local actors will capitalize on the issues of race, politics, and law. The idea of a creditors committee, given this maelstrom, at least provides a single forum to hear these issues and gives a district's stakeholders an important opportunity to contribute to the state's intervention and possible takeover.

Bankruptcy also differs in what happens *after* the rehabilitation plan. First, chapter eleven bankruptcies rarely involve a trustee.[17] Instead, the debtor customarily holds broad discretion to operate the business during a bankruptcy.[18] This differs from takeovers because the trustee's analogy, the appointment of a state administrator, is routine. Trustees in bankruptcies are appointed only when, as shown by clear and convincing evidence, the debtor commits fraud, dishonesty, incompetence, or gross mismanagement.[19] Despite its focus on bad deeds and gross mismanagement, this standard resembles the takeover standard. A takeover's measuring bar is usually the joint failures of satisfactorily meeting takeover criteria and not implementing an improvement plan. Because a failure to implement an improvement plan is reasonably explained by district officials' bad deeds or inability to implement the plan (similar to gross mismanagement), the takeover bar is comparable.

A bankruptcy trustee has costs and benefits. Trustees remove local expertise, increase management expense, and result in delays while the new manager learns the ropes.[20] On the other hand, the trustee is uniquely able to bring antagonistic parties to work together where existing management could not.[21] The state administrator is similarly situated: uniquely able to forge compromise, but threatening to the local expertise required for district turnaround. Chapter 4 explores this conundrum in more detail.

Second, bankruptcies often result in the appointment of an *examiner*. Courts can choose to appoint an examiner as an alternative to a trustee, either by request of a party (and after evidence is presented) or because debts exceed $5 million.[22] The examiner investigates allegations of fraud, dishonesty, incompetence, misconduct, mismanagement, or irregularity in the management of the debtor's affairs.[23] The standard for appointing examiners is lower than for trustees, loosely resembling the audits or reports often mandated by states prior to a takeover. However, examiners act differently than audits because they target bad actors or actions (fraud, dishonesty, misconduct, or irregularities), suggesting that these examiners gather information to determine whether a trustee should be appointed.

AN EXIT STRATEGY

Bankruptcies have an exit strategy in case of failure: the corporation's liquidation. Corporate property is converted to cash and the cash is distributed to creditors.[24] More than 80 percent of chapter eleven bankruptcies exercise liquidation as an exit strategy.[25] That is, even after reorganization, the vast majority of bankruptcies fail and must liquidate. Bankruptcy prospects are grim despite a clear, contentiousless standard, a freely entered-into contract, and profit-motivated stakeholders.

The high rate of chapter eleven bankruptcy failures should disturb state takeover policymakers. If these bankruptcies have predictive value, states takeovers will result in many more failures than successes. While this failure rate seems high, the very few takeover examples cited as successes certainly point to a similar proportion of failures. What distinguishes the bankruptcy and takeover failure rates, however, is that state takeovers have no exit strategy. A few states authorize a school district's annexation or dissolution after takeover, but, as discussed above, neither has been attempted. Consequently, state takeovers last indefinitely. Takeovers in Newark and Jersey City, New Jersey, are more than a decade long, while the one in Compton, California, is approaching a decade.

To summarize, the bankruptcy analogy suggests several important points. First, the apt analogy is to chapter eleven (or corporate) bankruptcies, where creditors look to future earnings as takeover actors focus on future academic achievement. Second, these bankruptcies have a few structures that state takeovers might emulate: clear criteria, creditors' committees, an examiner, and an exit strategy. Third, the appointment of a trustee is rare in bankruptcies and, when appointed, the trustee adds expense in removing local expertise and benefits in his or her ability to bring antagonistic parties together. Fourth, and most importantly, bankrupt corporations who enter rehabilitation plans more often than not fail and must liquidate. This last point should sober educational policymakers who fearlessly enter the treacherous waters of takeovers.

The danger of treacherous waters, however, does not preclude innovation. The next two chapters present a model for state intervention in failing school districts. Chapter 3 develops a framework for state intervention before an outright takeover, while chapter 4 explores outright takeovers.

NOTES

1. Atul Gawande, "When Good Doctors Go Bad," *The New Yorker* (Aug. 7, 2000): 60.

2. See Amy Berk and Anne Lewis, "Academic Bankruptcy," a policy brief from the Ed. Comm. of the States (1997). See also Margaret Dolan, "State Takeover of a Local School District in New Jersey: A Case Study," *Consortium for Pol'y Res. in Educ. Res. Report Series TC-008* 7 (1992) (quoting first state takeover advocate who said that bankruptcy was the model for intervention).

3. Chris Pipho, "State and Local Control: Rainbow and Dark Clouds," *Phi Delta Kappan* 6 (Sep. 1998).

4. David Epstein et al., *Bankruptcy* 8 (1992).

5. Takeover statutes in Texas (Tx St §39.131(10)), Iowa (Iowa St §256.11(12)), Arkansas (Ark St §6-20-1609), and Oklahoma (Ok St §1210.541(9)) authorize such annexations.

6. See Epstein et al., *Bankruptcy* 8 (1992).

7. See Epstein et al., *Bankruptcy* 8 (1992).

8. Hamid Tavakolian, "Bankruptcy: An Emerging Corporate Strategy," *Adv. Mgt. J.,* (Mar. 22, 1995): 18.

9. Tavakolian, "Bankruptcy: An Emerging Corporate Strategy."

10. See Paul Rosynsky, "State Finally Begins Takeover of Emery School District," *Oak. Trib.* (Jan. 12, 2001) (School board votes to enter state control in exchange for financial bail-out.). See also Lee Mueller, "Floyd Board OKs Longer State Takeover of Its Schools," *Lex. Her.-Leader* (Jan. 23, 2001) (School board voted to extend state control for another three years.).

11. See Epstein et al., *Bankruptcy* 12–13 (1992).

12. See Epstein et al., *Bankruptcy* 12–13 (1992): 759–61.

13. Josh Martin, "Down But Not Out," *Mgt. Rev.* (Dec. 1, 1999).

14. There are examples of CSSOs, school boards, mayors, and legislators negotiating interventions, but these examples are exceptional. See Ron Stodghill,

"Mayors Rule the Schools," *Time* (Apr. 12, 1999): 74 (describing Chicago, Ill., intervention); Caroline Hendrie, "Plan to Allow Mich. School Takeover Hailed," *Ed. Wk.* (Feb. 12, 1997): 15 (describing Detroit, Mich., intervention); Beth Reinhard, "Mayor to Get School Control in Cleveland," *Ed. Wk.* (Jul. 9, 1997): 1 (describing Cleveland intervention); Jessica Portner, "Plan Tying Increased Aid, State Control of Baltimore Schools Backed," *Ed. Wk.* (Apr. 16, 1997): 21 (describing Baltimore intervention).

15. See Epstein et al., *Bankruptcy* (1992): 750–51
16. See Epstein et al., *Bankruptcy* (1992): 751–52.
17. See Epstein et al., *Bankruptcy* (1992): 13.
18. See Epstein et al., *Bankruptcy* (1992): 740.
19. See Epstein et al., *Bankruptcy* (1992): 746.
20. See Epstein et al., *Bankruptcy* (1992): 747–48.
21. See Epstein et al., *Bankruptcy* (1992): 747–48.
22. See Epstein et al., *Bankruptcy* (1992): 748–49.
23. See Epstein et al., *Bankruptcy* (1992): 748.
24. See Epstein et al., *Bankruptcy* (1992): 8.
25. See Hamid Tavakolian, "Bankruptcy: An Emerging Corporate Strategy," *Adv. Mgt. J.* (Mar. 22, 1995): 18.

3

AN INNOVATIVE FRAMEWORK

In the simplest of takeover prologues, fifteen districts in Kentucky entered the final warning stage before a takeover.[1] Thirteen returned to normal status, while the state board of education formally charged Floyd and Whitley counties.[2] Thirty days later, an administrative hearing approved the Floyd takeover.[3] These events demonstrate a key principle: a takeover statute's success relies on improving districts that are not taken over, for example, the thirteen school districts that returned to normal status. Because the takeover process is inevitably difficult and the results uncertain, the proper target of a takeover regime is district improvement absent takeover.

A statute's framework, at minimum, must reflect this principle. It should do so through two supports. The first, a "soft" support, is the relationship between district and state. The second, a "hard" support, is the set of criteria prompting intervention, demarcating intervention stages, and evaluating progress through the stages. This section explores both supports, while the policy specifics of actual takeovers are deliberated in chapter 4.

THE STATE–DISTRICT RELATIONSHIP

The state can help improve a school district's performance, but it cannot bear the full burden of improvement. The appropriate image is the state as a spotter. A tired weightlifter and attentive spotter, for example, can easily lift what cannot be lifted solely by the weightlifter. A spotter who intervenes a moment too late, however, endangers the sapped weightlifter, while a too-early intervention results in a distrusting, un-dertrained weightlifter. State interventions face a similar dilemma. A too-early intervention will provoke a district's hostility, while a too-late intervention may strain beyond the state's ability to help.

An interventionist state can take either a collaborative or an authori-tarian approach. An authoritarian approach emphasizes authority under law, and diminishes the authority granted to local professionals.[4] A col-laborative approach emphasizes power sharing and problem solving.[5] For example, a collaborative improvement plan is developed in concert between local and state actors, while an authoritarian one is imposed upon the district by the state.

The logic behind an authoritarian state is understandable. The state's authority to intervene is prompted by a failing school district. A district's teachers and bureaucracy help to explain this failure, so the state has been given authority to replace the district's bureaucracy with its own. Combine this broad power with frustrating local actors and suffering children, and an authoritarian state attitude seems natural.

But a state's authoritarian, command-and-control approach is anath-ema to a productive takeover regime. While fairness is an issue,[6] a state's authoritarian approach has proved mistaken because it impedes the very end sought by the state: district improvement. In the pretakeover stage, only school district officials and personnel can do the heavy lifting of dis-trict improvement, making this approach a recipe for ineffectual lead-ership.[7]

Franchise businesses offer another analogy that cautions against an au-thoritarian approach. The analogy likens the school district to a franchisee, for example, the local McDonald's, and the state to the franchiser, for ex-ample, McDonald's central administration. Control and monitoring are im-portant and contentious features of the franchise relationship, as they are in state–district relations. Franchising research is nearly unanimous in es-

tablishing that command-and-control techniques are counterproductive to the success of a franchise.[8] Productivity instead relies on a collaborative decision-making process, with consensual relations reducing strife and dissension.[9]

State takeover statutes and their implementation do not in practice fit tidily into authoritarian or collaborative boxes. Indeed, a new state administrator, a revamped strategy, or new local conditions have produced mid-course changes in state–district relations.[10] Nor does authoritarian legislation lead inexorably to authoritarian implementation. For example, although possessing statutorily defined authoritarian powers, the Massachusetts's CSSO brokered a deal with the local school board in Lawrence, Massachusetts's. The state opened an office at the school district to oversee daily operations and provide technical assistance.[11] A deputy commissioner made it clear: "It is important to express this as a cooperative agreement."[12] The state worked with and not over local actors.

Recommending a collaborative state–district relationship is easy; structuring collaboration is more difficult.

THE STRUCTURE

Three features should shape a takeover regime: (a) improvement in struggling districts absent a takeover, (b) collaboration and negotiation, and (c) a strategy informed by takeover experiences. Constructing the "hard" support of a takeover's structure with these features in mind results in recommendations for the criteria prompting intervention, the stages of intervention, and standards for evaluating progress through the stages.

Criteria

A deterrence scheme based on status, in which a district is put on probation, depends on standards for judging a district's performance. These criteria, as most analysts agree, should be a broad range of indicators that reflect the quality and effectiveness of a school district's educational program.[13]

Practicality argues that the choice of these criteria be influenced by lessons from takeover experiences. If takeovers in the past have improved a particular district function, including that function in takeover criteria is sensible. If a district fails to improve that function, the ensuing takeover has a good prospect for improvement. But if the record on takeovers shows an inability to improve a particular district function, including that function in criteria is a formula for failure. The district will likely fail to improve it, and so will a state takeover.

Two criteria point to district functions that the state can improve: the overhead ratio (administration/student expenses) and the measure of facilities. Takeovers have proven that state intervention can result in dollars moving away from central offices and to classrooms. Therefore, a high overhead ratio may suggest a school district where a takeover may work. Similarly, because takeovers have resulted in facility improvements, a measure for the condition of district facilities is sensible.

This is not to argue only for financial and facility measures. Test scores are typically relied on by state legislatures to judge school-district performance. For example, Ohio's statute offers eighteen criteria; seventeen of those are test-based.[14] These scores at least partially reflect pupil achievement in district schools, thus their incorporation is necessary. Reliance only on test scores, however, besides ignoring the varied functions a school district performs, sets up a state takeover for failure because takeovers have shown a limited effect on test scores.

A significant measure missing from most takeover statutes is capacity building. These investments initially show little affect in district performance, but have long-term results. Examples of capacity building measures are investments in professional development, school-based reforms, or district reorganization. A broad-based criteria scheme should anticipate these long-term results by measuring short-term investments in capacity.

The state has an opportunity to involve school districts in the choice of criteria, the setting of failure rates, and the number of failing criteria that trigger intervention. To make decision-making collaborative, franchises use an advisory-council organization of franchisees to shape franchise policy.[15] Similarly, school districts should help develop the criteria that states use to trigger intervention. By ensuring that a high percentage of low-performing school districts are represented in such a council, the state goes a long way toward producing buy-in and commitment, and toward reassuring that it is not acting in a command-and-control mode.

School district officials should influence, either by a convening or a statewide committee, the actual percentages that trigger intervention. For example, these officials may choose the dropout rate as one of the takeover criteria, then fix a dropout rate higher than 10 percent as unsatisfactory, and identify failing districts as those who are unsatisfactory in 50 percent or more of the criteria.

The Process

Different rationales operate more or less vigorously during the intervention stages. The deterrence rationale operates at full strength during the early stages of intervention, while by the time of an outright takeover, state-led district improvement is the primary rationale. Consistent, meaningful, and practical criteria are essential in this effort. Targeted sanctions and public shaming, explored later in this chapter, are important elements, too. In addition, the state should take affirmative action, as a spotter does, to help lift district performance. Finally, as a school district fails to adequately improve, the state must rely on its considerable leverage to negotiate district change.

The school board and superintendent drive management and/or operational improvements. By increasing pressure on district leadership, pressure for improvement increases throughout the educational service chain, i.e., pressure on the school board and superintendent results in more effective administration, principals, and teachers. Therefore, the district's leadership must be at the center of a sanctions scheme. *Public shame* and *fear of job loss* are the sanction methods, providing the necessary pressure while also sending a strong message to other struggling school districts.

Local newspaper, television, and radio coverage of state intervention is the default method of public shaming. As one administrator explained, it goes to a basic human motivation: no one wants his or her work labeled as failing.[16] Moreover, school boards are particularly susceptible to public shame since they are often elected. Superintendents are similarly wary of shaming because it threatens their current authority and future job prospects.

States have shown little tactical intelligence in their use of public shaming, choosing to rely instead on the traditional media to communicate a district's failing status. A more tactical approach, for example, would broaden the audience. Through the use of community meetings, the state should underscore the message of district failure to churches, nonprofits, local politicians, businesses, and activists. Or the state can target informational mailings to district parents, voters, and businesses. Whether by direct contact or blanket public relations, the state can spur these constituencies to pressure district leadership.

In addition, tactical shaming may instigate the community to take up the task of improving pupil achievement. For example, a state takeover in Detroit, Michigan, drew the support of 150 local churches.[17] It is not unreasonable to believe that, after tactical shaming of the school district, these churches would have been motivated to start an educational improvement initiative, such as an after-school homework program.

Job loss is a more direct mechanism of deterrence aimed at district leadership. The fear is clear-cut for the district's superintendent since a takeover usually results in his or her replacement. Improvement is the sole means for keeping his or her job. Because board members are often relegated to advisory status with a takeover (rather than replacement), the connection is less clear-cut. The electoral system provides a route for direct pressure on board members. For example, Missouri's statute permits a recall election for board members,[18] which probably produces heightened accountability.[19] As an alternative, the state can delegate the power to appoint school board members to a mayor, as happened in Chicago and Boston.

The state should complement its public shaming and job threats with affirmative help for the school district. The logical vehicle for improvement is a collaboratively created improvement plan, written locally and incorporating input from state-appointed experts. Its focus should be singular: improving the district's performance on the criterion that prompted intervention. Capacity-building criteria should attract particular attention. These measures—the results of which are not easily captured in the first few years—are a rough measure of a district's commitment to progress. Because capacity building requires extra funding, state financial assistance is absolutely necessary at this stage.

The state has an additional goal during this intervention stage. To prepare for future negotiation or takeover, the state should collect information and develop relationships with important actors. First, the CSSO should appoint an independent external evaluator akin to bankruptcy's examiner position. The external evaluator scrutinizes the district's non-improvement in case-study fashion. Political and institutional climate, history, demographic changes, and union–district relations all play a role in this evaluation. Further, the examiner reports on all the factors relevant to a potential takeover, including focus groups or surveys of the district's parents and teachers. This report should be made available to the district, parents, and teachers. Although its analysis is pertinent to the improvement plan, the evaluation should serve primarily as a strategic document for the CSSO to chart an intervention's course.

The CSSO faces a quandary in appointing an external evaluator: Should the external evaluator be compelled to identify local actors who frustrate district improvement? The "naming names" dilemma, faced by other crisis and intervention models,[20] has costs and benefits. Naming names empowers the leadership to weed out frustrating actors, possibly board members, a superintendent, or high-level administrators. On the other hand, naming names creates an atmosphere where the flow of information to the evaluator is restricted, for fear of being named. Traditional audits do not name names, so there is little comparative evidence from which to base a recommendation.

Second, the state should establish an Intervention Advisory Board. Like a creditors' committee in bankruptcy that assembles concerned players, the board increases the flow of information to the state and builds relationships with important local actors. Pennsylvania's 2000 takeover statute crafts such an intervention advisory board.[21] To aid in the improvement plan's development, the board is composed of a school board member, the superintendent, the district's business manager, a teacher, two parents, a businessperson, a local community leader, and two general public members. While a great start, the Pennsylvania board is weighted too heavily toward district personnel and does not represent the full panoply of district stakeholders.

An improved intervention advisory board should include, in addition to the board members above, the mayor, other locally elected officials, a neighboring district's superintendent, and local community leaders. In its spirit of collaboration, this board creates buy-in from potential stakeholders, allays fears of an authoritarian state attitude, and provides a distinctly local perspective on the state intervention.

This board could also serve as a venue for any capacity-building efforts spurred by state intervention, such as whole school reforms or private–public partnerships.

Evaluation Standards

With these building blocks in place, the next step is to evaluate a district's progress. Performance on takeover criteria is the ideal measuring stick, helping to keep a district resolutely focused on achievement related to the underlying criteria. But performance on takeover criteria should not be the near-term measuring stick. First, as even the most successful of takeovers show, academic improvements lie dormant for at least three to five years.[22] Fairness commands that school districts not be held to a higher standard of improvement than that shown by actual state takeovers. Second, takeover criteria overlook short-term investments that may lead to subsequent improvement. For example, substantial investments in teacher training will probably not show up in test scores for several years.

As mentioned earlier, an improvement plan should be tailored to increase district performance related to takeover criteria and should include short-term investments for future improvement. Therefore, implementation of the plan is an approximate gauge of a district's future improvement. It is a necessary and an admittedly second-best answer for measuring a school district's effort in the first several years of intervention.

There is a pitfall to using the improvement plan as a short-term measuring stick for district improvement. With any process-based measurement, there is a temptation to gauge implementation by compliance, in which perfunctory compliance becomes the goal. To defend against this likelihood, the state should place a high value on a district's concrete action in relation to the improvement plan.

In addition to the implementation of the improvement plan, two sets of criteria should be used as short-term measuring sticks. Many takeovers have shown substantial improvement in facilities and finances within the first few years. Districts should be held similarly accountable for facility and financial results within the first several years of intervention.

One principle should predominate during intervention: resistance requires dramatic state action, while a district lacking the capacity to achieve an objective requires further assistance. Evaluation of the improvement plan provides a good vehicle for this principle. A school board or superintendent who resists implementing the improvement plan must trigger immediate and further intervention or state control, for example, public shaming or a recall election for a recalcitrant board member. On the other hand, a school board or superintendent who attempts to implement the plan but lacks the capacity or expertise must trigger immediate help.

This evaluation structure presents a difficult scenario. Suppose a school district implements its improvement plan but, after five years, fails to improve on the underlying takeover criteria. A takeover sounds inappropriate. After all, the state's help with and approval of the improvement plan casts doubt on whether the state as district operator would perform any better. But two explanations for this discrepancy counsel for a state takeover. First, the improvement plan may not have been implemented as successfully as the state measured. Second, corruption or patronage (or similar endemic problems) may be so rooted in the district that any improvements as a result of the improvement plan were countered. Under either scenario, a takeover or further intervention is necessary.

In summary, the measuring stick during a state intervention changes over time. Two measurements should be employed during the first several years of an intervention: implementation of the improvement plan and progress on facilities and finance measures. After that, the only standard is improvement on takeover criteria. Throughout the process, individual or wholesale resistance should provoke further intervention. District improvement on takeover criteria should not end state intervention; rather, continuing in its role as spotter, the state stands ready to help or intervene further if progress halts. A state intervention should diminish only when the school district is no longer failing according to takeover criteria. Chapter 4 recommends a state strategy when districts are no longer failing.

Heightened Intervention

A district's failure to improve or a district's resistance to state intervention should provoke a heightened intervention. A failing school district must feel the full weight of a statutorily authorized takeover, resulting in a maximum of state leverage. Despite the authority, this is not a time to leap the chasm to takeover without a hesitation—in other words, take the proverbial look before the leap. The state at this point has the leverage to tip a compromise solution for district improvement. Thus, negotiation is the key method for this stage.

Aggressive interventionists will argue that the district has been given enough time and that delay only strengthens those who frustrate improvement. While a call for action is understandable, the state must remind itself of the alternative. State takeovers have a spotty record at best, and anything short of state control that achieves district improvement is, as much for the state as the district, a bullet dodged.[23] Local officials, driven by a fear of a takeover's stigma, and state officials, facing imminent responsibility for a task they are unsure they can *really* tackle, should embrace options beside takeover.

Negotiation is more likely than outright takeover to result in exactly what is needed for improvement: buy-in from many stakeholders. Surprisingly, while CSSOs, school boards, mayors, and legislators negotiated interventions in Chicago,[24] Detroit,[25] Cleveland,[26] and Baltimore,[27] these examples are far from customary. Negotiated outcomes can result in increased mayoral influence (or control); university–district partnerships; a restructuring of district policy, leadership, or finances; and/or state control in individual areas of school district affairs.

The Intervention Advisory Board is a natural vehicle for negotiation. It brings together state and local officials, and actors from within and outside of the educational field. Of course, as a bankruptcy expert earlier cautioned, these additional voices may spook the horse.[28] But, if prior takeover experiences have any predictive value, a unilateral takeover will spook it, too. Better to negotiate and win allies in the process than to jump into being responsible for a soon-to-be spooked horse.

This chapter creates an improved intervention structure. By focusing on effective, meaningful criteria and by thinking strategically about job loss and public shaming, the state uses deterrence to encourage district improvement absent a takeover. By avoiding an authoritarian, command-and-control approach and embracing collaboration and negotiation, the state does well to achieve the desired improvement, again, without a takeover. Yet some school districts will not improve during state intervention. A small share of these will resist a negotiated outcome, thereby prompting a takeover. The next chapter offers best practices for this stage.

NOTES

1. Patricia Fry et al., "Kentucky's Program for Educationally Deficient School Districts: A Case Study," *Consortium for Pol'y Res. in Educ. Res. Reports* (1992): 15–18.

2. Fry et al., "Kentucky's Program."

3. Fry et al., "Kentucky's Program."

4. See David Mayrowetz and James Pennell, "A Naturalistic Inquiry of Envisioned Worlds: Conceptualizing and Classifying State Intervention Laws," *Amer. Educ. Ass'n Res. Paper* (1997): 16.

5. Mayrowetz and Pennell, "A Naturalistic Inquiry," 17.

6. School districts in disadvantaged neighborhoods face a more difficult task than others because of the social, political, and cultural problems in these neighborhoods. An authoritarian approach explains the locality's failure by lack of effort, talent, or corruption by district staff, rather than addressing the conditions that may produce failure.

7. See generally David Kirp and Cyrus Driver, "The Aspirations of Systemic Reform Meet the Realities of Localism," *Ed. Admin. Q.* 31 (1995): 589 (describing the quadrupling of the California education code yet still no real power of the state over school districts).

8. Andrew C. Seldan, "Recent Academic Research Points the Way to More Effective Franchise Agreements," *Leader's Franchising Bus. and L. Alert*, (Apr. 2000): 1.

9. Seldan, "Recent Academic Research."

10. See Charles Mahtesian, "Whose Schools?" *Governing Mag.* (Sep. 1997): 34.

11. Robert Johnson, "Lawrence, Mass., Reaches Deal with State," *Ed. Wk.* (Feb. 4, 1998): 3.

12. Johnson, "Lawrence, Mass., Reaches Deal with State."

13. See Thomas Gusky, "Policy Issues and Options When States Take over Local School Districts," *Int'l J. of Educ. Reform* 2 (1992): 68, 70.

14. OH ST §3302.02-.04; OH Admin Code §3301-15-03 to –05

15. Seldan, "Recent Academic Research," 1.

16. See Mary Skelly, "A New Jersey Success Story," *Sch. and College* 28, no. 11, (1989): 11.

17. See Tracy Van Moorlehem, "School Takeover Bid Gets Endorsements," *Det. Free Press,* (Feb. 27, 1999): A8.

18. Missouri St. §160.538(5)(a)

19. The recall solution is an example of an innovative alternative to the collaborative or authoritarian approaches. Termed a *democratic approach,* it reinforces the authority of a school district's residents and professional educators by delegating authority back to local actors. David Mayrowetz and James Pennell, "A Naturalistic Inquiry of Envisioned Worlds: Conceptualizing and Classifying State Intervention Laws," *Amer. Educ. Ass'n Res. Paper* 7 (1997).

20. See Martha Minow, "Between Vengeance and Forgiveness," (1998): 86–87 (explaining the decision of whether international humanitarian commissions should name perpetrators).

21. 24 Penn. St. § 17-1703B(d)

22. See Jack Leonard, "Compton, State School Officials Seek Truce," *L.A. Times* (Oct. 6, 1998): B1 (academic improvement after five years of intervention); Richard Burr, "State Takeovers Display Mixed Education Results," *Det. News,* (Feb. 9, 1997): B5 (academic improvements in the third year after the state delegated authority to the mayor).

23. See Jessica Sandham, "Despite Takeover Laws, States Moving Cautiously on Interventions," *Ed. Wk.* (Apr. 14, 1999): 21 (citing state officials increasing caution in takeover matters).

24. See Ron Stodghill, "Mayors Rule the Schools," *Time,* (Apr. 12, 1999): 74 (describing Chicago, Ill., intervention).

25. See Caroline Hendrie, "Plan to Allow Mich. School Takeover Hailed," *Ed. Wk.,* (Feb. 12, 1997): 15 (describing Detroit, Mich., intervention).

26. See Beth Reinhard, "Mayor to Get School Control in Cleveland," *Ed. Wk.* (Jul. 9, 1997): 1.

27. See Jessica Portner, "Plan Tying Increased Aid, State Control of Baltimore Schools Backed," *Ed. Wk.* (Apr. 16, 1997): 21 (describing Baltimore intervention).

28. See David Epstein et al., *Bankruptcy* (1992): 751–52.

4

EXECUTING TAKEOVERS:
A LAST RESORT

Takeovers exist within bleak, inopportune waters. One superintendent likened the state's pursuit of a takeover to "a dog chasing a car. Once a dog catches it, he's not sure what he's going to do with it."[1] The state is forced to deal with many issues, both predictable and not: "You'll pick up a piece of paper to examine an issue and find a huge quagmire underneath."[2] At the extreme of implementation problems, a shot was fired at a state administrator in Compton, California.[3] Though less sensational, a school district's politics and culture inevitably challenge (and sometimes defeat) a state's efforts.[4]

This section begins to suggest a navigable route through these waters, offering lessons for leadership and management, replacing the board and superintendent, assessing staff, providing assistance, nurturing local alliances, and the state's exit.

LEADERSHIP AND MANAGEMENT

The takeover in Compton, California, demonstrates the strength and weakness of state-run leadership. On the one hand, the last Compton state administrator is viewed as one of the most successful takeover leaders ever.[5] An African American raised in inner-city Boston, Dr. Randolph Ward effectively combined charisma with a degree from Harvard, fluency in Spanish, and experience as an administrator in a neighboring district.[6] On the other hand, eight years of state control produced five different state administrators,[7] with one surviving for only four months.[8] During the early years of the Compton takeover, resistant actors could bet on changes surviving only as long—or as short—as the current administrator's term.

The state must provide consistent, high-quality leadership. If it cannot, the state fails to answer the institutional choice question: what does it offer beyond the locality? The takeover in Letcher County suggests Kentucky offered little. The state interviewed only eight candidates—all *principals* from neighboring districts—for the position of state administrator.[9] On the other hand, Illinois hired a highly regarded administrator for East St. Louis who had displayed parallel skills in moving a good-sized local hospital from the brink of disaster to financial stability.[10]

In unilaterally taking over a local school district, the state faces an uphill struggle to avoid being *autocratic*. A state administrator is predisposed toward autocratic leadership because of the job's temporary status and severe goal pressure,[11] and, with the school board removed or in advisory capacity, the usual check on an autocrat is missing. An autocratic leader encourages edicts and isolation, while a superintendent with a desire to persuade encourages two-way communication.[12]

In addition, research on franchisor–franchisee relations concludes that management guided by command-and-control is counterproductive.[13] This style is particularly ineffective with takeovers because it exacerbates existing tensions: racial, outsider–insider, legal, and so on. Compton's second superintendent provides an example. The superintendent's motto in a previous district had been "Turn up the heat!"[14] Needless to say, teachers' unions in both places vehemently opposed his leadership.[15]

An authoritarian state attitude during a takeover inevitably creates conflict. A researcher of the Jersey City, New Jersey, takeover describes the psychology:

> Co-optation, symbolic response, non-compliance, resistance, and alienation describe the attitude of many Jersey City locals to the takeover. . . . With-

out sufficient support, the extreme pressure applied by the state resulted in an environment characterized by poor timing and unreasonable timelines, insider-outsider conflicts, the politics of waiting, unreasonable and unmet expectations, and poor communication.[16]

Heavy-handed tactics doom a takeover from the start.

Nonautocratic leadership worked in a Chicago takeover. The key, according to the president of the local teacher's union, was cooperation between superintendent, mayor, and the union.[17] For example, while authorizing the takeover, the Illinois legislature eliminated the district's grievance-and-negotiation procedures that were part of the district's collective bargaining agreement.[18] Nevertheless, after a takeover, the mayor-appointed administrator passed the same worker protections as before as a matter of board policy.[19]

A state takeover should lead to a focus on schools. The state intervenes to improve student achievement and that requires improved services at the school level.[20] To achieve a focus on schools, individual classrooms and schools must see change. Kentucky's first-year legislative requirements produced a leadership focused almost entirely on compliance and administrative reorganization, resulting in Letcher County's schools never feeling the state's presence.[21] A parent complained, "If they start dealing with instructional problems—things like whether they have adequate textbooks and whether teachers are qualified to teach their courses—the people will come to see state intervention as a positive thing."[22]

Transferring dollars saved from better management into classrooms is good policy. It answers the parent's criticism and is a highly visible demonstration of a focus on schools. In Cleveland, Ohio, the superintendent fired thirteen central-office staff members and transferred the savings directly to district schools.[23] In Newark, New Jersey, the $26 million saved through reorganization bought instructional supplies.[24]

There is a shortcut to a focus on schools: choose one area and fix it. For example, after a couple of years of mediocre results in six taken-over schools, New York City schools' chief fired school principals, adopted Success for All in failing schools, and a year later, reading scores at each school rose.[25] Other alternatives include class-size reductions or a promise that every student receives a textbook for every class.

Teachers find a focus on schools especially important. Many teachers in taken-over districts feel threatened by a constant pressure for better test scores.[26] Teachers will look more favorably on state intervention—and its inevitable pressure for higher test scores—if the state can show that new funds or programs are entering schools.

Early successes greatly benefit leadership.[27] The state can positively market these successes (and the intervention itself) to the local community and create momentum for district improvement. For example, participants agreed that a key explanation for West Virginia's takeover success in Logan County was its strategy: identify eight to ten fixable problems per year, and fix only these problems.[28] A parent criticized the Jersey City, New Jersey, takeover for missing this point: "Why are they going whole hog. . . . Why couldn't they have done it gradually? Move in first and try to deal with the money—trim that down. Then maybe fix special education and as they clean-up each closet move on to the next closet."[29] Two takeover experiences suggest targeting one type of fixable problem: facilities. In Jersey City, a year of intervention resulted in cleaner buildings,[30] while Dr. Randolph Ward's first year in Compton resulted in two hundred leaky roofs fixed.[31]

Timelines are anathema to effective leadership and management. A timeline for the length of takeover only caters to staff and administrators willing to play the "politics of waiting"—where the insiders patiently wait until the outsiders exit.[32] The means for state exit must be criteria-based, sending the message to resistant staff that only district improvement will result in state exit. In Paterson, New Jersey, it took several months before administrators and the community realized that the state was not exiting any time soon. After this sank in, the takeover became less susceptible to the political ax.[33]

REMOVING AND REPLACING THE SCHOOL BOARD AND SUPERINTENDENT

The state must confront a question that, although deeply implicated in effective leadership and management, gives rise to its own set of concerns: what should be the role, if any, for the local school board and superintendent? The state's decision to retain, remove, or replace the

school board and superintendent determine whether state–district relations will be authoritarian or collaborative. Outright replacement of
both parties is squarely authoritarian, and as mentioned earlier, probably invites unnecessary conflict. A collaborative model probably results
in an advisory board. A democratic solution, as mentioned in the last
section, is to initiate new local elections for the school board.

An uncooperative board may produce a takeover's proverbial dagger-
in-the-back, yet an active, cooperative school board can help improve a
district. After all, the school board is a repository of institutional knowl-
edge and an important community connection.[34] For example, in the
takeover in Logan County, West Virginia, most participants found the
board essential to the takeover's success.[35] While retaining ultimate authority, the state administrator regularly adapted policy after consulting
with the board.[36] On the other hand, retaining the school board creates
a fuzzy sharing of power with the state; for this reason, legislators in
Connecticut dissolved Hartford's school board.[37]

The standard for removal or replacement recalls the distinction between resistance and capacity covered in the former section. A school
board that actively resists state policies warrants removal or replacement, while a board that does not possess the wherewithal to implement
a policy should be assisted.[38] Since this distinction cannot be made without giving the board a chance after a takeover, no takeover should be im-
mediately followed by school board removal. Keeping the board in advisory capacity is preferable.

The same analysis does not apply to the district's superintendent,
where replacement has several benefits. First, the state secures itself as
the day-to-day driver of the district's operations and leadership. Second,
removing a superintendent puts board members on notice that they may
be next. Third, this strategy avoids a probable legal action for a voting-
rights violation.

If resistance occurs, the school board should be removed and re-
placed after several last efforts. Two examples suggest initial outlines for
these efforts. First, Kentucky developed an agreement with the Letcher
County school board not to pursue misconduct charges against board
members on the condition that board members were forthcoming in
terms of state involvement.[39] This artful agreement should have de-
terred future misconduct or noncooperation, while still preserving the

board as a contributor. Unfortunately, the intervention wound up in court for unrelated reasons, leaving the agreement's effectiveness unknown. Second, Iowa's takeover legislation requires the state and local school board to form an intervention agreement. The legislation presses local board members to be reasonable because, absent an agreement, a receiver will be appointed or the district will be merged with another.[40] But the pressure is not one-sided. The state is—or should be—wary of jumping into the takeover thicket and should prefer a mutual arrangement short of a takeover.

ASSESSING AND REMOVING STAFF

Takeovers often result in firings or their threat, usually directed at central office staff and principals. In Logan County, W. Va., principals were told their jobs depended on improving test scores.[41] Thirty-eight central office staff in Compton, California, lost their jobs following a state takeover,[42] as well as seventeen in Paterson, New Jersey.[43] Layoffs or their threat breed suspicion and mistrust. State officials see only misdeeds; meanwhile, staff members see only slights. On the other hand, layoffs expunge a school district of old employees and infuse it with new, hopefully more productive ones. One administrator argued that layoffs were a prerequisite: "I'm not sure you can improve a district under the leadership that has brought it down."[44]

Three issues are central to firings or their threat. First, principals and staff may retain tenure or bump-down rights. New Jersey's original takeover bill eliminated these rights, but the teachers' union fought hard to get them reinstated in the final bill.[45] As a result, Paterson's state administrator was forced to negotiate many settlements to remove personnel from the district.[46] Some personnel in another Jersey City's school district used tenure rights, which, according to one takeover analyst, created a reshuffling instead of a reorganization.[47]

The second issue is timelines. Both in Kentucky and New Jersey, takeover legislation set a timeline for evaluating staff and principals. Staff officials in New Jersey had to assess principals and staff members within six months.[48] These evaluations consumed precious time and resources because the state, reluctant to end up in court, had to be careful not to violate employees' due-process rights.[49] Yet neither Kentucky's nor New Jersey's program successfully rooted out the old guard.[50]

Institutional memory is the third issue. The layoff threat may make staff edgy and restrict the flow of information to takeover officials. District improvements, which often involve complex processes, cannot begin without information flowing swiftly to the state. Just as with bankruptcies, the removal of experienced staff can become a stumbling block. This block only intensifies when district employees traditionally use informal lines of communication.[51]

Remedies to these issues are found partly in better legislation and partly in better implementation. State officials should possess the power to assess and remove district staff and principals; otherwise, state officials face needless exposure to uncooperative staff, the "politics of waiting," and the possibility of resistant forces finding shelter in bumping down or tenure rights. Legislators should be willing to bargain with teachers' unions, offering, if necessary, additional funding or programs in exchange for support.

However, while states should possess the statutory power to assess and remove staff, it should be hesitant to do so. Uncooperative staff or members playing the "politics of waiting" should be fired. Evaluating principals, arguably the most important manager in the process of delivering educational services, should garner immediate attention because of their pivotal role in pupil achievement.[52] But to initiate change, the state must grasp the current state of affairs, and in this effort, imminent layoffs and "purges" are anathema. They aggravate the state's understanding of current affairs and consume time better spent on management and leadership efforts.

ASSISTANCE

Some analysts believe that a takeover's success depends, not on leadership or management, but on extra financial assistance.[53] The state typically provides technical assistance during takeovers, but most legislation and takeover experiences involve no extra funding. In Jersey City and Paterson, New Jersey, no extra money was provided nor was there a mechanism to raise additional funds;[54] while in Letcher County, Kentucky, a paltry $20,000 came with intervention.[55] On the other hand, Maryland provided Baltimore's district with an extra $254 million over five years.[56] Pennsylvania's takeover regime is the only to require financial support; state-run districts are assisted by a $450,000 grant.[57]

Extra funding is necessary for three reasons. First, takeovers are difficult enough without some funding cushion, particularly in districts with large financial deficits. Second, as part of the strategy to nurture local alliances (discussed below), extra funding may allay fear and gain support among teachers' unions and parents. To parents, extra money implies that students may receive better services as a result of state intervention. To teachers, extra money implies that the state is not placing blame solely on them. Further, teachers' unions find takeovers absent financial assistance hard to digest—an executive director of a large teacher's union in Wisconsin criticized a proposal for a Milwaukee takeover precisely because the state offered no additional assistance.[58] Third, financial assistance funds capacity-building projects. Allying the district with a local teaching college, or creating a more competitive teacher's salary scale, or adopting a whole school reform requires money, and several years may pass before cost savings and reorganization bear financial fruit.

NURTURING LOCAL ALLIANCES

Given the cherished concept of local control, it is surprising how often teachers, politicians, and local communities either support or do not oppose state takeovers. In Detroit, several teachers' unions and three major community groups, including the Detroit Association of Black Organizations, supported a takeover.[59] In Whitley County, Kentucky, teachers were happy to see the state's arrival,[60] and in Chicago, Illinois,[61] and Hartford, Connecticut,[62] teachers' unions at least did not oppose takeovers. In Paterson, New Jersey, the mayor supported a takeover,[63] while the community was relieved by the takeover in Hartford, Connecticut[64]

State officials should gain the support of parents and teachers. Getting these constituencies on board helps deflect a takeover's racial overtones, creates necessary buy-in for affecting serious reform, and may be a necessary element for capacity building.[65] Parents have children who suffer a failing district. A focus on schools and positive marketing (discussed below) are strategies to gain parents' support. Teachers also receive the day-to-day brunt of corrupt, ineffectively managed schools. A focus on schools is central to getting teachers' support and, at the very least, getting teachers' support also means not cutting teachers' salaries. Exemplifying the poorest of strategies, some takeovers were quickly followed by teacher's salary cuts.[66] If the state desires academic improvements, then alienating teachers, those most closely associated with pupil achievement, is flawed policy.

State interventions should also reach out to local leaders. Local leaders may find personal and public satisfaction from being a part of a district reform effort. In Chicago and Detroit, the state ceded management and control of city schools to the mayor. A Detroit mayor explained how this arrangement may indeed be the most reasonable by institutional choice standards: "Any mayor in the country will tell you that the No. 1 issue facing cities isn't crime or jobs anymore, it's public education. Mayors have every reason to take on the responsibility."[67] Mayors are also key players in capacity building, possessing crucial community connections, financial resources, and the requisite skills to organize.

Positive marketing is an important front in the battle to improve a school district. Marketing first requires using the right language. State officials should term state involvement as an intervention and not a takeover.[68] While intervention connotes extra aid or involvement, a takeover connotes war and is bound to provoke an emotional response. Second, the state must promote. For example, the state administrator in Jersey City placed thousands of large signs reading, "Jersey City Public Schools—Kids First," in all district buildings within three days of takeover.[69] Staff and parents received a bumper sticker with the same slogan, while a local company paid for similar postings around the city.[70]

Compton, California, provides a telling example of what happens when the state makes no effort to promote its intervention. Several years into a takeover, and after little outreach to the community, the state campaigned for a local bond measure to fund badly needed capital improvements in the schools.[71] Angry at the takeover, the local mayor rallied opposition and defeated the bond. District repairs totalling $107 million went undone.[72]

THE STATE'S EXIT

A staged return to local control should begin only when the district is no longer deficient, judging by the same criteria and standards that prompted intervention. Using a different set of criteria for a state takeover, rather for than state intervention, suggests disparate treatment of the state and school district.[73] Also, to fight a return of the old guard, the district should remain eligible for immediate state intervention in the three years following. In Jersey City, New Jersey, the state appointed and trained local residents as board members. Due to the rough-and-tumble nature of electoral politics, when local control returned, these residents lost elections to the same ex-board members whose administration spurred state intervention.[74]

If progress stops, the state's re-intervention should be quick and sufficient. Compton's return to local control, which began in October 2000, provides an example. The state rates the district in five areas (facilities, finances, pupil achievement, personnel management, and community relations) on a ten-point scale. When a six is reached in an area, the school board is granted limited authority to manage that area.[75] Only after the district scores a 7.5 average in each area is full control returned, but even then a state trustee retains oversight powers for two years.[76]

This chapter provides a guide for the most treacherous part of any takeover statute: an outright takeover. It guides the state away from rocky shores, like the automatic removal of the school board, and toward safe waters, like providing financial assistance. By no means do these practices guarantee a successful takeover. They represent an experience-based best course.

SUMMARY

Constructing a takeover regime requires careful navigation. State actors contemplating their intervention options should consider when and how it can best help. Timing, strategy, and common sense are essential. Takeover discourse should focus mostly on lessons learned from a decade of takeover experiences. But other crisis and intervention models—like bankruptcy and franchising—should not be neglected.

There are four broad lessons for state takeovers of local school districts: (a) The state's authority is best used as a deterrent, (b) the state should focus on what it knows it can affect, (c) inept districts require state assistance, while wrongdoing ones require intervention, (d) the state, acting as a political animal, should collaborate and negotiate.

This last point should be stressed. My central thesis is that command-and-control behavior—states' traditional approach during takeovers—is poor strategy. It fuels opposition, does little to allay the locality's fears, and frustrates progress. Instead of acting as an occupying army, the state should reconceptualize its role as a powerful lever, pushing for better management and leadership within the district and expanding a school district's capacity to educate its students.

These broad lessons translate into many policy choices. The following list summarizes these choices.

A Takeover Model: Policy and Practice

1. Takeover Criteria
   Consistent and Varied Criteria, Focusing on Improvable Phenomenon
   • Multiple performance indicators, including test scores, capacity-building efforts, facilities, and financial measures (overhead ratio)
   • Advisory council of school district officials, in which underperforming districts are overrepresented, to revise or set values for these criteria

2. Intervention
   Improvement Plan: Collaborative, Nonauthoritarian, Capacity-Building Approach
   • Local team to develop plan with expert assistance from state
   • Extra funding
   • Pressure on district leadership
   • Public shaming and/or job loss
   • External evaluator—conducts an independent case study of district's failure, including political and institutional climate, history, demographic changes, and union–district relations
   • Intervention advisory board—composed of district officials, locally elected officials, and community leaders; provides external

analysis of district's failure and a forum for capacity-building possibilities

3. Evaluation
   A Shifting Standard for Further Intervention
   • Within the first three years: Is the improvement plan being implemented? Are facilities and finances improved?
   • After three years: Has the district performance on takeover criteria improved?
   • If resistance, heightened intervention; if lack of capacity, further assistance

4. Heightened Intervention
   Full Takeover Is Last Resort
   • State uses negotiation to achieve the improvement plan's goals, involving mayor, governor, teachers' unions, and the community through the intervention advisory board
   • If negotiation fails, state assumes control

5. Takeover
   School Leadership and Administration
   • School board in advisory capacity; state administrator replaces superintendent
   • If school board or individual member is uncooperative, remove board or member or hold recall election
   • Eliminate tenure and "bump-down" rights of central office staff and principals
   • Focus evaluation on principals
   • Nurture local alliances
   • Market positively to community
   • Reach out to parents and teachers
   • Provide financial and technical assistance
   • For capacity-building programs
   • Realizable, concrete gains at the school level
   • State administrator reports yearly on how state intervention affects individual schools
   • Transfer saved dollars to schools

6. State Exit
   Fair Criteria and Protect Gains
   - When no longer deficient by the same criteria that prompted intervention
   - Three-year window after local control for swift state intervention

FUTURE DIRECTIONS

While *Navigating Treacherous Waters* fills a pressing need by advocating for a model takeover's policy and practice, three important questions remain unanswered. First, does the deterrent effect of takeover regimes spur improvement in districts in jeopardy? An empirical study is needed to assess the effect of a takeover regime on non-taken-over school districts. If a deterrent effect exists, the general failure of takeovers to improve academic performance takes on a different gloss: this failure is a regrettable but necessary byproduct of generally improving educational performance. If no effect exists, the remaining rationale for takeover statutes is severely challenged, because evidence of takeovers' effect on academic improvement in state-controlled districts is murky at best.

Second, after an unsuccessful state takeover, what should happen next? Recall that, if bankruptcies hold any comparative value, the majority of takeovers will fail. Some states offer a school district's dissolution or annexation as an exit strategy. While logically appealing, these options are untried and a major departure from standard procedure. To develop an appropriate exit strategy requires more research and careful thought.

Finally, the question remains: are state takeovers a good idea? The question can have one of three answers: takeovers are good policy, or good policy implemented poorly, or plain bad policy. Legislators certainly have made up their minds that takeovers are good policy and show no signs of slowing their tide. I assume the second proposition, but only for the practical reason that, if takeovers are a *de facto* policy tool, educational policymakers and practitioners ought to create a new, smarter type of takeover regime. If takeovers are bad policy, state policymakers can either retreat from meddling in school districts, or find a more effective method of meddling. The latter option is ripe for original thinking.

NOTES

1. James Salazar, "Legislation Looks to Send out Rescue Teams to Save State's Schools, *Athens News* (Nov. 29, 1997): A2.

2. Michael Rettig, "Policy Adaptation and Change: The Case of the State Takeover of Jersey City Public Schools," *Amer. Educ. Res. Ass'n paper* (1992): 25

3. Lori Olszewski, "School District Takeovers Take Off," *S.F. Chron.* (Apr. 14, 1999): A17.

4. Eloise Forster, "State Intervention in Local School Districts: Education Solution or Political Process," *Amer. Ed. Res. Ass'n Paper* (1996): 16–17.

5. Joe Matthews, "States to End Takeover of Compton Schools," *L.A. Times* (Sep. 18, 2000): 1.

6. Matthews, "States to End Takeover."

7. Kevin Bushweller, "Under Shadow of the State," *The Amer. Sch. Board J.* (Aug. 1998): 17–18.

8. Jeff Leeds, "2 Top School Officials in Compton Quit Education," *L.A. Times* (Jul. 18, 1996): B3.

9. See Mark Schaver, "Letcher County Board to Let State Take over Schools," *Courier J.* (Louisville, Ky., 1994): B1.

10. Margaret Gillerman, "Firm to Oversee Finances of E. St. Louis Schools," *St. Louis Post-Dispatch* (Nov. 3, 1994): B1.

11. Michael Rettig, "Policy Adaptation and Change: The Case of the State Takeover of Jersey City Public Schools," *Amer. Educ. Res. Ass'n paper* 28 (1992).

12. Rettig, "Policy Adaptation."

13. See Andrew C. Seldan, "Recent Academic Research Points the Way to More Effective Franchise Agreements," *Leader's Franchising Bus. and L. Alert* (Apr. 2000): 1.

14. Howard Blume, "Raising Compton's Bottom Line: New Administrator Has a History of Turning Scores and Heads," *L.A. Times* (Mar. 10, 1994): 8.

15. Blume, "Raising Compton's Bottom Line."

16. See Rettig, "Policy Adaptation and Change."

17. "CTU President Says Union Was Key to Real School Reform," *The PFT Reporter* (Phil. Federation of Teachers) at www.pft.org/02.html (accessed Dec. 1, 2000).

18. "CTU President."

19. "CTU President."

20. In fact, legislation in California and Kentucky favors school—and not district—takeovers. See California's Public Schools Accountability Act of 2000; and Fry et al., "Kentucky's Program for Educationally Deficient School Dis-

tricts: A Case Study," *Consortium for Pol'y Res. in Educ. Res. Reports* (1992): 25. Taken to its extreme, some takeover statutes permit the state to reconstitute individual schools. Beth Reinhard and Caroline Hendrie, "At Two Cleveland Schools, Overhauls Mark a Dramatic Response to 'Desperate Times,'" *Ed. Wk.* (Sep. 24, 1997): 13.

21. See Susan Fuhrman and Richard Elmore, "Takeover and Deregulation: Working Models of New State and Local Regulatory Relationships." *Consortium for Pol'y Res. in Educ. Res. Report* 27–28 (1992).

22. Mark Schaver, "Letcher School Board Suspended by Boysen," *Courier J.* (Louisville, Ky.), (May 17, 1995): A1.

23. "Mayor White Fired 13 School Officials," *News5 Net* (Oct. 2, 1998) newsnet5.com/news/stories/news-981002-170807.html (accessed Apr. 6, 2002).

24. See Laura Litvan, "States Try to Rescue Schools," *Investor's Bus. Daily* (Feb. 17, 1998): A1.

25. See Nicholas Lehman, "'Ready, READ!' A New Solution to the Problem of Failing Schools Is Emerging," *Atl. Mnthly,* (Nov. 1998): 92–104.

26. See, e.g., Susan Fuhrman and Richard Elmore, "Takeover and Deregulation: Working Models of New State and Local Regulatory Relationships," *Consortium for Pol'y Res. in Educ. Res. Report* 13 (1992).

27. The corollary is also true: the state must avoid early disasters. In New Jersey, the redesign of a purchasing system in the first year of takeover became a disaster that hurt state authority. Rettig, "Policy Adaptation and Change," 30.

28. Bushweller, "Under Shadow of the State," 17.

29. Rettig, "Policy Adaptation and Change," 36.

30. Rettig, "Policy Adaptation and Change," 17.

31. Matthews, "States to End Takeover," 1.

32. See Rettig, "Policy Adaptation and Change," 25–26.

33. See Rettig, "Policy Adaptation and Change," 24.

34. This is true in other contexts, too. In ex-communist countries, reform-minded leaders confront a related problem with generals and police chiefs of the old regime who say: "We can harm you a lot if you remove us, and help you a lot if you retain us." "Is It Changing Fast Enough," *Economist* (Nov. 11, 2000): 63.

35. See Bushweller, "Under Shadow of the State," 17.

36. See Bushweller, "Under Shadow of the State," 17.

37. Jeff Archer, "Connecticut Bill to Seize Hartford Schools Passes," *Ed. Wk.* (Apr. 23, 1997): 30.

38. Fuhrman and Elmore, "Takeover and Deregulation," 6.

39. Schaver, "Letcher School Board to Let State Take over Schools," *Courier J.* (Louisville, Ky., 1994): B1.

40. IA St § 256.11 (12).

41. See Litvan, "States Try to Rescue Schools," A1.

42. Howard Blume, "More Job Cuts, Demotions Ordered in Failing District," *L.A. Times,* (Aug. 12, 1993): 1.

43. Laval Wilson, "Takeover: The Paterson Story," *Amer. School Board Jour.* (Dec. 1994): 23.

44. Olszewski, "School District Takeovers Take Off," A17.

45. Margaret Dolan, "State Takeover of a Local School District in New Jersey: A Case Study," *Consortium for Pol'y Res. in Educ. Res. Report Series TC-008* 8 (1992).

46. Wilson, "Takeover: The Paterson Story," 23.

47. See Dolan, "State Takeover of a Local School District," 31.

48. See Dolan, "State Takeover of a Local School District," 21.

49. See Dolan, "State Takeover of a Local School District," 24.

50. Fuhrman and Elmore, "Takeover and Deregulation," 30.

51. See Dolan, "State Takeover," 15.

52. See generally John Chubb and Terry Moe, *Politics, Markets, and America's Schools,* Brookings Institution, 1990, 84–86.

53. Richard Hunter and Jeff Swann, "School Takeovers and Enhanced Answerability," *Ed. & Urb. Soc'y* 31 (1999): 238, 251

54. Dolan, "State Takeover of a Local School District," 27.

55. Bushweller, "Under Shadow of the State," 17.

56. Jessica Portner, "Plan Tying Increased Aid, State Control of Baltimore Schools Backed," *Ed. Wk.* (Apr. 16, 1997): 21.

57. 24 P.S §17-1709-B.

58. Reinhard, "Thompson Threatens a Takeover," 14.

59. Tracy Van Moorlehem, "School Takeover Bid Gets Endorsements," *Det. Free Press* (Feb. 27, 1999): A8.

60. See Fry et al., "Kentucky's Program," 17.

61. See Ron Stodghill, "Mayors Rule the Schools," *Time* (Apr. 12, 1999): 75.

62. See Jeff Archer, "Connecticut Bill to Seize Hartford Schools Passes," *Ed. Wk.* (Apr. 23, 1997): 30.

63. See David Berman, "Takeovers of Local Government: An Overview and Evaluation of State Policies," *Publius* (Jun. 22, 1995): 66.

64. Archer, "Connecticut Bill," 30.

65. See generally Paul Hill, "Helping Hands," *Brookings Rev.* 18 (Jul 1, 2000): 3, 18.

66. For example, Compton teachers received a 10.5 percent pay cut after a takeover. Howard Blume, "More Job Cuts, Demotions Ordered in Failing District," *L.A. Times* (Aug. 12, 1993): 1.

67. See Stodghill, "Mayors Rule the Schools," 74.

68. See Charles Mahtesian, "Whose Schools?" *Governing Mag.* (Sep. 1997): 34–38 (noting that takeover participants in New Jersey and Ohio prefer intervention over takeover).

69. Dolan, "State Takeover," 15.

70. Dolan, "State Takeover," 15.

71. Matthews, "States to End Takeover," 1.

72. Matthews, "States to End Takeover," 1.

73. See, e.g., Mahtesian, "Whose Schools?" at 34–38 (A state's exit, as described by one observer: "Eventually, I imagine they'll lower the bar, declare victory and get out.")

74. See Laval Wilson, "Takeovers Work," *Amer. School Board J.* 19 (Aug. 1998).

75. Matthews, "States to End Takeover," 1.

76. Matthews, "States to End Takeover," 1.

INDEX

Arkansas, 15n29

bankruptcy, 21–28; creditors' committee in, 24–25; criteria for, 23; examiner in, 25–26; exit strategy, 26–27; failure, high rate of, 26–27; liquidation under, 22–23, 26; process of, 24–26; trustee in, 25; types and purposes of, 22–23
bureaucracy: Republican governors' distrust of, 4

California, 4, 39n7; Compton, 1, 8, 9–10, 11, 12, 26, 41–42, 44, 46, 49, 50, 56, 56n66
capacity building. *See* school district, capacity of
chief state school officer (CSSO), 2, 3
community, 34; alliances with, 48–50; groups, 48; marketing to, 44, 49; parents, 43, 48
Connecticut: Hartford, 2, 45, 48

corrective action plan. *See* improvement plan
courts. *See* law

decentralization, trend toward, 4
deterrence, 5–6; job loss, fear of, 7, 33, 34; research in, 53; shame, 5–6, 15n29, 33; stigma, 23

"effective schools" literature, 4
equal opportunity, 4
exit strategy, 26–27, 44, 50, 53, 57n72

facilities. *See* school district, facilities
finances. *See* school district, finances
franchise, 30, 42

governors, 4, 5, 6, 11

Illinois: Chicago, 2, 12, 34, 38, 43, 48, 49; East St. Louis, 42

ABOUT THE AUTHOR

Liam J. Garland works for the city of Oakland, California, as an attorney serving low-income neighborhoods. Prior to this, he taught elementary school as a Teach for America corps member in the taken-over school district of Compton, California, and provided legal services in San Francisco jails.

He has a bachelor's degree in government from Cornell University and a law degree from Boalt Hall School of Law, University of California at Berkeley. In 2002, he published *Getting to the Table,* a primer about gaining community benefits from union-only project labor agreements.

He and his wife, Tina Trujillo, live in Oakland, California.